Baltimore County
— Maryland —

OVERSEERS OF ROADS

1693-1793

Henry C. Peden, Jr., M.A.

HERITAGE BOOKS
2008

HERITAGE BOOKS
AN IMPRINT OF HERITAGE BOOKS, INC.

Books, CDs, and more—Worldwide

For our listing of thousands of titles see our website at
www.HeritageBooks.com

Published 2008 by
HERITAGE BOOKS, INC.
Publishing Division
100 Railroad Ave. #104
Westminster, Maryland 21157

Originally published 1992

All rights reserved. No part of this book may be reproduced or transmitted in any form or by any means, electronic or mechanical, including photocopying, recording or by any information storage and retrieval system without written permission from the author, except for the inclusion of brief quotations in a review.

International Standard Book Numbers
Paperbound: 978-1-58549-217-6
Clothbound: 978-0-7884-7735-5

FOREWORD

The opening and clearing of roads and the maintenance of bridges were of major concern and importance to colonial Baltimore Countians. They needed to get their goods to market in all kinds of weather. And the need for travel extended beyond commercial endeavors into both public and private reasons.

Consequently, men of good standing were called upon to oversee existing roads and to open new ones periodically as ordered by the county court. The appointments of overseers of roads are recorded in the minutes and proceedings of the Baltimore County Court. The description of the territory covered by each overseer gives us some very valuable information that is useful in genealogical research. It not only identifies the men themselves and places them at a specific location and time, but it also lets us know about many of the inhabitants who lived in the area. Many references are made to natural geographical features such as rivers (or falls), streams and ridges, as well as man-made roads, mills, and bridges.

The information contained in this book has been taken from the original records at the Maryland State Archives in Annapolis, Maryland, as pertains to Baltimore County, namely Proceedings Libers G; IS #A; GM; IS #C; IS TW #1-#3; HWS 6, 7, 9; HWS #IA; TB & TR; TB #D; BA #1-#2; TB & TR #1; TR #5-#6; BB #A; BB #B; and, Minute Books #1-#5 (plus 2 unnumbered books) for the years 1693 trough 1793. It should be mentioned that proceedings began in 1682, but a review of these early books revealed no appointments of overseers. However, due to the rather poor quality of these books and their flowery and difficult to read print, some early appointments may have been overlooked in the books for the years 1682 to 1692. Likewise, no overseers were found from 1697 to 1707, and proceedings for 1726, 1727, 1748, 1749, 1752, 1753, 1764, 1766, 1767, 1770, 1771, 1773 and 1774 are not extant.

To assist in locating the places cited within this book a map of Baltimore County circa 1773, prepared by William B. Marye for his article entitled "The Old Indian Road" (See *Maryland Historical Magazine*, Vol. XV, No. 2, pp. 107-123, June, 1920), has been inserted. The reader is well advised to consult Mr. Marye's article for more descriptive details.

After 1773, Harford County was separated from Baltimore County, and in 1837 Carroll County was formed from parts of Baltimore County and Frederick County.

Henry C. Peden, Jr.
Bel Air, Maryland
June 1, 1992

BALTIMORE COUNTY OVERSEERS OF ROADS, 1693-1793

THOMAS HOOKER appointed overseer of highways instead of George Norman, who is ordered dismissed - November, 1693.

EDWARD BOOTHBY was presented by Robert Drisdel for not appearing at the highways and by the Grand Jury the said presentment was "Returned Ignoramous" - November, 1693.

GEORGE SMITH appointed overseer of highways for Spesutie Hundred - November, 1694.

THOMAS CORD appointed overseer of highways for Spesutie Hundred - November, 1694.

WILLIAM LENOX appointed overseer of highways for Gunpowder Hundred - November, 1694.

WILLIAM HORNE appointed overseer of highways on the south side of Gunpowder Hundred - November, 1694.

JOHN BROAD appointed overseer of highways on north side of Patapsco Hundred - November, 1694.

ROWLAND THORNBOROUGH appointed overseer of highways for the lower part of Patapsco Hundred - November, 1694.

JOHN LOTWOOD [?] appointed overseer of highways for the south side of Patapsco Hundred - November, 1694.

"The Court empowers all overseers to have at their disposal every tithable in their respective area to help them with clearing and maintaining of the roads." - November, 1694.

ANTHONY DREW appointed overseer of highways for Spesutie Hundred - November, 1695.

LAWRENCE RICHARDSON appointed overseer of highways for south side of Gunpowder Hundred - November, 1695.

FRANCIS ROBINSON appointed overseer of highways on the south side of Gunpowder Hundred near Back River - November, 1695.

[Note: There are no proceedings from 1697 through 1707].

MATHEW ORGAN, planter, appointed overseer of highways for the Upper Division of north side of Patapsco - November, 1708.

WILLIAM DENTON, planter, appointed overseer of highways for the south side of Gunpowder Hundred - November, 1708.

GEORGE WELLS, gentleman, appointed overseer of highways for the Upper Division of Spesuty Hundred - November, 1708.

HENRY BUTLER, carpenter, appointed overseer of highways from Gwins Falls into Jones Falls and for the back roads between said falls - November, 1709.

THOMAS HUTCHINS, planter, appointed overseer of highways on south side of Gunpowder Hundred - November, 1709.

GEORGE CHAUNCY, gentleman, appointed overseer of highways in the room of William Pritchard - November, 1709.

JOHN HARRYMAN appointed overseer of highways in the room of William Wilkinson - November, 1709.

TEAGOE TRACY appointed overseer of highways in the room of Tobias Starnsboro - November, 1709.

JOHN BUCK, planter, appointed overseer of highways in the Upper Division of south side of Patapsco in the room of John Greeniff [?] - November, 1709.

ROGER MATHEWS appointed overseer of highways for the Lower Division of Spesuty Hundred in the room of George Chancy - November, 1710.

JOHN STOKES appointed overseer of highways for the Upper Division of Spesuty Hundred in the room of George Wells - November, 1710.

RICHARD SAMSON appointed overseer of highways in the room of John Harriman - November, 1710.

WILLIAM BOND appointed overseer of highways in the room of Henry Donnahue - November, 1710.

ROBERT GORSUCH appointed overseer of highways from Hurst [Hursh?] Falls to the head of Bare Creek and to the Herring Run - November, 1710.

JOHN ARSMTRONG appointed overseer of highways in the room of James Preston, Jr. - November, 1710.

AMBROSE NELSON, JR. appointed overseer of highways in Lower Hundred on south side of Patapsco in the room of Thomas Croker - November, 1711.

JOHN GALLION appointed overseer of road that leads from the rolling house of John Hall, Esq. to his upper quarters - November, 1711.

"We of the Jury for our Sovereign Lady and the Body of this County do desire that the present overseers of Spesuty Hundred highways may be ordered to clear all the roads within each respective precinct to be well cleared before they be discharged from their offices." Signed by William Howard, foreman - November, 1711.

ANTHONY BALE appointed overseer of highways in Lower Division of Spesuty Hundred in the room of Roger Mathews - June, 1712.

JOHN BROWN appointed overseer of highways in Upper Division of Spesuty Hundred in the room of John Stokes - June, 1712.

GEORGE GROVER appointed overseer of highways on south side of Gunpowder Hundred in the room of James Durham - November, 1712.

THOMAS BOND appointed overseer of the "Land of Nod" roads in the room of William Bond - November, 1712.

LANCELOT TOD appointed overseer of highways on south side of Patapsco Hundred in the room of Thomas Cromwell - November, 1712.

LAWRENCE DRAPER appointed overseer of highways in Upper Division of Spesuty Hundred instead of John Brown - November, 1713.

WILLIAM ROBINSON appointed overseer of highways in Lower Division on south side of Patapsco River instead of Ambrose Nelson - November, 1713.

WILLIAM FORREST appointed overseer of highways in Lower Hundred on south side of Patapsco River instead of Lancelot Tod - November, 1713.

SIMON PEERSON appointed overseer of highways in north side of Gunpowder Hundred instead of John Armstrong - November, 1713.

WALTER BOSLEY appointed overseer of highways in south side of Gunpowder Hundred - November, 1713.

PETER LESTER appointed overseer of highways in Lower Division of Spesuty Hundred instead of Anthony Bale - March, 1713.

JOHN GILL appointed overseer of highways in Upper Hundred on north side of Patapsco River instead of Henry Butler - March, 1713.

JOHN CARTER appointed overseer of highways in Lower Hundred on north side of Patapsco River - March, 1713.

GEORGE PECKET appointed overseer of highways from the White Marsh to Brittain Ridge - August, 1714.

EDWARD KANTWELL appointed overseer of highways in Lower Division of Spesuty Hundred - March, 1714.

JOHN WILMOT appointed overseer of highways of Back River Hundred in the room of Thomas Cannon - November, 1715.

SAMUEL ARDEN appointed overseer of highways in Lower Division of north side of Patapsco in the room of Richard Samson, deceased - November, 1715.

FRANCIS WHITEHEAD appointed overseer of highways in south side of Gunpowder in the room of William Colleson - November, 1715.

JONATHAN TIPTON appointed overseer of the forrest road leading from the Garrison Ridge by the Widow Stephenson to the White Marsh, and all the inhabitants on Garrison Ridge and Little Brittain are to assist in clearing and marking same - June, 1716.

WILLIAM WRIGHT appointed overseer of highways on south side of Gunpowder Hundred - November, 1716.

CHARLES ROCKHOLD appointed overseer of highways on south side of Patapsco - November, 1716.

JOHN FITSREDMAN appointed overseer of highways in Back River Hundred - Novemner, 1716.

LAWRENCE TAYLOR appointed overseer of highways in Upper Part of Spesutie Hundred - November, 1716.

WILLIAM OSBOURN appointed overseer of highways in Lower Part of Spesutie Hundred - November, 1716.

PHILLIP WASHINGTON appointed overseer of highways in Lower Hundred on north side of Patapsco - November, 1716.

"On the petition of Thomas Hughs to have a road to his house from Patapsco Ferry Landing through the plantation of Nicholas Fitsimonds, it is ordered that Peter Bond and John Israel lay out a road to the said Hughs's house as convenient as may be with the least detriment to the said Fitsimonds." - June, 1717.

JOHN ROBERTS appointed overseer of highways in the hundred on south side of Gunpowder - November, 1717.

JOHN WILLING appointed overseer of highways in Back River Hundred - November, 1717.

JOSHUA COCKEY appointed overseer of highways for Spesutie Hundred - November, 1717.

ROBERT JACKSON appointed overseer of highways in the Hundred on north side of Gunpowder - March, 1717.

MARK WHITTAKER appointed overseer of the rolling road from Deer Creek to the rolling house of John Hall, Esq., and the other roads from said creek to the main road through the county or to the water - June, 1718.

THOMAS TOLLEY appointed overseer of highways in south side of Gunpowder Hundred instead of John Roberts - November, 1718.

JOHN EAGER appointed overseer of highways in Lower Hundred on the north side of Patapsco - November, 1718.

JOHN NEWSOME appointed overseer of highways in Lower Part of Spesutie Hundred - November, 1718.

WILLIAM COOKE appointed overseer of highways in Upper Part of Spesutie Hundred - November, 1718.

JOHN ASHMAN appointed overseer of highways on south side of Patapsco in the Lower Hundred - November, 1719

SAMUEL HINTON appointed overseer of highways in Lower Hundred on the north side of Patapsco - November, 1719.

STEPHEN GILL appointed overseer of highways in the Upper Hundred on the north side of Patapsco - November, 1719.

JOHN HILLEN appointed overseer of highways instead of Thomas Weeks for Back River Hundred - November, 1720.

RICHARD OWENS appointed overseer of highways between the Main Falls of Patapsco and Gwins Falls, and ordered to clear a new road to and over Gwins Falls - November, 1720.

JOSEPHUS MURRAY appointed overseer of highways between Gwins Falls and Jones Falls instead of Stephen Gill - November, 1720.

LUKE STARNSBURY appointed overseer of highways in Upper Part of Back River Hundred above the main road - November, 1720.

THOMAS GORSUCH appointed overseer of highways in the Lower Hundred on north side of Patapsco - August, 1721.

JOSEPH FREEMAN appointed overseer of highways in the Lower Hundred on south side of Patapsco - August, 1721.

EDMOND TALBOTT appointed overseer of highways in the Lower Part of the hundred on north side of Gunpowder - August, 1721.

"Ordered that a road from the south side of Patapsco Ferry Landing be cleared to the house where Thomas Hughs dwelleth along the stand but that the same be not done till the last day of November next." - August, 1721.

SAMUEL HUGHES appointed overseer of roads for the Upper Part of Spetutia Hundred instead of John Gallion - November, 1722.

GEORGE DREW appointed overseer of the highways for the Lower Part of the Lower Division of Spetutia Hundred - November, 1722.

EDWARD HALL appointed overseer of roads for the Upper Division of Spetutia Hundred - November, 1722.

ROGER MATHEWS appointed overseer of roads for the Upper Division of Spetutia Hundred - November, 1722.

BENJAMIN HOWARD appointed overseer of highways for the Lower Part of Elk Ridge Hundred (below Deep Run) - March, 1721.

JOHN NORTON appointed overseer of the Lower Hundred of the north side of Patapsco River - June, 1722.

HENRY BUTLER appointed overseer of public roads between Gwinn's Falls and Jones's Falls - November, 1723.

EDWARD HARRIS appointed overseer of roads in the Upper Hundred of Spesutia and it is ordered that he clear the same as Mr. Edward Hall, late overseer, should have done - November, 1723.

LUKE TROTTEN appointed overseer of roads in Patapsco Neck - November, 1723.

JOHN WISELY appointed overseer of roads in Lower Division of the Hundred on the north side of Gunpowder River - June, 1724.

THOMAS WRIGHT appointed overseer of roads in the Lower Devition on the south side of Patapsco River - November, 1724.

RICHARD GOTT appointed overseer of roads in Britton Ridge - November, 1724.

THOMAS STANSBURY appointed overseer of roads in lower part of Back River Hundred - November, 1724.

THOMAS BURCHFIELD appointed overseer of roads in the lower precincts of the Lowest Devition in Spesutia - November, 1724.

"The Court ascertains that several roads in Baltimore County into several districts and to each district an overseer is appointed." - August, 1728.

JOHN DURBIN appointed overseer of the main road on the west side of Binam's Run by William Bradford's to the Upper Ferry on Susquehannah River to the rolling roads leading to Esquire Hall's rolling house from Deer Creek, the road from Deer Creek to Mr. Edward Hall's plantation, and a road from John Webster's to St. George's Parish Church to be cleared according to Mr. William's Smith's directions - August, 1728.

EDWARD HALL appointed overseer of the main road from Susquehannah River Ferry to Binam's Run, and also the church road from Susquehannah aforesaid - August, 1728.

WILLIAM COOK appointed overseer from the main road at the end of Edward Hall's plantation to the Red Lyon Bridge where the old church stood, from thence over the long bridge to St. George's Parish Church, and from thence to the Rev. Stephen Wilkinson's at the Glebe - August, 1728.

GEORGE DREW appointed overseer of road from Humphry's Run to said Drew's, from Mr. Aquila Hall's to the Red Lyon Bridge, and from Rumley Bridge to Mr. Roger Mathews - August, 1728.

WILLIAM BOND appointed overseer of the several rolling roads leading to Dr. Middlemore's landing, from Mr. Daniel Scott's towards the court house as far as Winter's Run, and the road leading from the Land of Nod to the mill at Winter's Run - August, 1728.

CHARLES SIMMONS appointed overseer of all the rolling roads leading to Mr. Paca's Mill landing, and the road from Winter's Run to Joppa Town - August, 1728.

AQUILA MASSEY appointed overseer of the main road from Binam's Run to the Little Falls of Gunpowder River, from said falls to Joppa, from Joppa to James Isham's, from Joppa aforesaid to Jonathan Massey's, and from the place called the Three Bridges at the head of a creek below William Burney's to Mrs. Paca's Mill - August, 1728.

THOMAS GIDDINGS appointed overseer of roads from the Little Falls to the Long Calm of the Great Falls, from thence to Nicholas Day's, from Thomas Hutchins' to the Little Falls and from Josias Hendon's to Luke Stansbury's Mill - August, 1728.

LUKE RAVEN, JR. appointed overseer of road from the Long Calm to Buffellow Branch, from said calm to Oliver Harriott's, from the head of Middle River to Esquire Dulaney's Quarter, and from the head of Middle River to "TL" - August, 1728.

THOMAS HARRIS appointed overseer of the main road from Buffellow Branch to the Herring Run at the head of Back River, and all other publick roads between the said branch and run - August, 1728.

WILLIAM BUCKNER appointed overseer of roads from Herring Run at the head of Back River to the Bayside and from Bayside up to St. Paul's Parish - August, 1728.

JOHN ENSOR appointed overseer of roads from Herring Run at the head of Back River to Jones's Falls, from said falls to the church, and from Britain Ridge rolling house to the extent of that hundred - August, 1728.

LUKE STANSBURY appointed overseer to clear a road according to law from the Long Calm of Gunpowder Falls to Edward Riston's plantation at Garrison's Ridge - August, 1728.

HENRY BUTLER appointed overseer of roads from Patapsco Ferry to Jones Falls at Mary Hanson's Mill, from said mill to Gwinn's Falls, from the same mill to Gwinn's Falls to the main falls above Christopher Randall's plantation, from the Garrison Ridge to the Rowling Landing at Gwinn's Falls and from said ridge to Mary Hanson's, the Church Road - August, 1728.

GEORGE BAILEY appointed overseer of roads from the lower fording place at the Main Falls of Patapsco as the main road now leads to Gwinn's Falls, from said fording place to Mole's Point, from same fording place to Ragland, from said Ragland to the ferry at Mole's Point aforesaid, from the Soldier's Delight to the landing at the head of Patapsco, from John Belt, Jr.'s plantation in the forest to said landing, from the Main Falls to Christopher Randall's to Gwinn's Falls where the road passes to the Widow Hanson's, and from Ben's Run by the plantation where Zebediah Baker now lives, to the aforesaid place at Gwin's Falls - August, 1728.

WILLIAM BURNEY petitioned the Court that the main road by his dwelling house door is a very great inconvenience to him and the frequent occasions of his being disturbed at unreasonable hours in the night. He requests that the road be turned about 100 yards on the backside of his dwelling house at his own expence and trouble. It was accordingly granted - August, 1728.

LOYD HARRIS appointed overseer of main roads from Herring Run at the head of Back River to Jones's Falls, from Jones's Falls to the church, and Brittain Ridge rowling road to the extent of that hundred for the ensuing year in the room of John Ensor - November, 1729.

WILLIAM MAINER appointed overseer of roads in the room of Thomas Broad - November, 1729.

SAMUEL DURBIN appointed overseer of roads from Thomas Johnson's down the main road that goes to Col. Holland's Quarter and from thence to the rolling house - March, 1729.

NICHOLAS DAY appointed overseer of roads in the room of Thomas Giddings from Little Falls of Gunpowder River to Luke Stansbury's Mill, from said Day's to the Long Calm and likewise from the same Day's to Picket's landing place, and from Thomas Johnson's to Thomas Hutchins' - March, 1729.

THOMAS LITTON appointed overseer of roads from Johnson's Ford where Deer Creek Road formerly came in to John Webster's rolling road, from Col. Holland's Ford to Esquire Hall's rolling house, and from Thomas Cullings' to Suquehannah Upper Ferry - June, 1730.

WILLIAM HAMMOND appointed overseer of road in the room of Daniel Rawlings between Gwins Falls and the Main Falls of Patapsco - June, 1730.

THOMAS FRANKLIN appointed overseer of roads in the room of Nicholas Day from Thomas Hutchins' to Luke Stansbury's Mill, from the Little Falls of Gunpowder River to the Long Green Bridge - June, 1730.

WILLIAM BOND appointed overseer of roads from Deer Creek Mill round Benjamin Wheeler's plantation until it intersects the Land of Nodd rolling road, which said roads are to be added to said Bond's former overseer's warrant - August, 1730.

THOMAS BURCHFIELD appointed overseer of roads from Level Bridge to Delph Bridge and also the road to Mr. Mathews' and the road over the Land [?] Bridge to the church - August, 1730.

WILLIAM HAMMOND appointed overseer of the highways in that part of the Patapsco Upper Hundred lying between the rolling road from the Soldier's Delight, Gwin's Falls to the landing, and all between the main road leading from Patapsco Falls inclusive of both said roads, and that he have the power to command Loyd Harrys, Charles Wells, and George Buchanan, their male taxables and half of Mr. Hocston's [?] hands that lye between the abovesaid two roads and the Main Falls of Patapsco - August, 1730.

WILLIAM HAMILTON appointed overseer of the highways between the main road from Patapsco Falls....Gwin's Falls, the rowling road from the Soldier's Delight to the landing and the Main Falls of Patapsco exclusive of both the said roads - August, 1730.

THOMAS LITTON formerly appointed overseer of roads about Deer Creek is now also overseer of the road that leads out of the rowling road to the head of Swan Creek, from the rowling road to the church, and from Thomas Cullin's to William Perkins' Landing - August, 1730.

GEORGE GARRETTSON appointed overseer of roads from Susquehannah Ferry to Humphry's Run and from the said ferry to the church - 1731.

"Court ordered a road be cleared between the main road and Moale's Point according as the same shall be laid out by two Justices, the said road to be cleared by the overseer of that precinct." - 1731.

EDWARD HALL appointed to remove the road through John Deaver's plantation to such convenient place as said Hall shall appoint - 1731.

CHARLES GORSUCH appointed overseer of roads from Herring Run to Patapsco Old Church, from said church to Walker's Mill and up Brittian's Ridge rolling road to Benjamin Bowen's Quarter and from said mill to said Herring Run - 1731.

JONAS ROBINSON appointed overseer of road between Patapsco Old Church and North Point - 1731.

ALEXANDER MACCOMAS appointed overseer of roads which Aquila Massey was overseer of the year past, and all other roads necessary to be cleared in that precinct - 1731.

ROBERT ROBERTSON appointed overseer to clear a road from Joppa to Henry [?] Mathews former landing where the ferry over Bush River is to be kept - 1731.

RICHARD WELLS appointed overseer of roads in the room of Thomas Litton of the upper part of Deer Creek, for the ensuing year - 1731.

WILLIAM SMITH appointed overseer of roads in the room of Thomas Burchfield from the Level Bridge to Delph Bridge and from thence to Mr. Roger Mathews and the road over the Long Bridge to the church, for the ensuing year - 1731.

JOSEPHUS MURRAY appointed overseer of the highways in the room of John Parrish between Gwins Falls and Jones's Falls, for the ensuing year - 1731.

JACOB GILES appointed overseer of roads from Zachariah Spenser's to the Rock Run, and from Thomas Phelps' to the said Rock Run and likewise from Susquehannah Fording to the Rock Run aforesaid - 1731.

"Court ordered that a road which leads through Philip Jones' plantation be turned round the same, upon the motion of said Philip Jones." - June, 1732.

LUKE TROTTEN, overseer of Patapsco Neck roads, is ordered to make sufficient "casways where such may wanting in the said roads." - June, 1732.

JONAS ROBERTSON appointed overseer of roads from Herring Run to the falls, and from said falls up Brittain's Ridge rolling road as far as usual - June, 1732.

BENJAMIN CADLE appointed overseer of roads in the neck of Gunpowder River, and is ordered to clear a road from the crossroads near Joppa to a plantation whereon Thomas Cross lives, according to the directions of Nicholas Day - November, 1733.

SAMUEL OWINGS appointed overseer of roads from Henry Butler's up by the Garrison to the North Run and from said Butler's by George Ogg's and James Wells' to Gwin's Falls, and rolling road from Edward Reeston's until it intersects the road from Walker's Mill to the said Butler's, and the Court Road from said Reeston's to Gwin's Falls - November, 1733.

"These inhabitants of Gunpowder Neck petitioned the Court that whereas the road leading down to Gunpowder Neck is altered and that we know no way except the old road without being obliged to go a mile out of our way crave that your Worships consider it be continued as formerly." Petition signed by Henry Wetherall, Aquila Massey, Gilbert Crockett, Thomas Tolley, William Hill, Jas. (Jos.?) Starkey, John Roberts, and Wells Stokes - November, 1733.

RICHARD JENKINS appointed overseer of roads of which George Garrettson was overseer, for the ensuing year - November, 1733.

JOHN ROGERS appointed overseer of roads of which Oliver Harriott was overseer, for the ensuing year - November, 1733.

NATHANIEL GIST appointed overseer of roads of which Henry Satyr was overseer, for the ensuing year - November, 1733.

CHARLES RIDGELY appointed overseer of roads in the room of Solomon Wooden from Walker's Mill to the ferry and Gwin's Falls and from said mill to Henry Butler's and from thence to Gwin's Falls aforesaid - November, 1733.

CHARLES WELLS appointed overseer of roads from Jones' Quarter to the Iron Works and the Indian Road out of said road to Gwin's Falls, out of said Jones' Road to Gist's Mill, from the Lower Wading Place of the Main Falls of Patapsco to the Second Wading Place of Gwin's Falls, from the Fording Place of Davis's Run to Moale's Point, from the Iron Works to William Hammond's, from the Lower Fording Place of Gwin's Falls to Moale's Point and the Ragland Roads that lead from the intersection of said road to said Moale's Point and that the overseer aforesaid warn half of Hyde's taxables and all of Buchanan's, Chapman's, Hurd's and Lewis' to work of said road - March, 1733.

CHRISTOPHER DUKE appointed overseer of roads in the room of Stephen Body from "TL" down into Back River Neck from Buffelow Branch to William King's Run - March, 1733.

CORNELIUS HOWARD appointed overseer to clear the roads from Gwin's Falls back of James Wells' up the fork of Gwin's Falls to Mathews' Cabin on Patapsco Falls and take the taxables on the north side of Soldier's Delight Hundred from Gwin's Falls to the Main Falls to clear the said roads, and that the said taxables be exempted from going on any other roads - June, 1734.

PERRIGRIN FRISBY appointed overseer of roads in the room of Abraham Cord in the Spesutie Lower Hundred - June, 1734.

WILLIAM WOOD appointed overseer of roads in the room of Charles Rockwell, for the ensuing year - June, 1734.

SAMUEL HOWELL petitioned the Court that he did, at his own expence, clear a road through his plantation from the main road leading to Susquehannah Lower Ferry, which road being convenient for travellers and the inhabitants thereabout, said Howell prayed the Worships to turn the main road through his plantation where he has cleared as aforesaid, the same being dry and the present main road being low and swampy. It was accordingly approved - June, 1734.

JOSEPH ALLEN appointed overseer of roads from the Levell Bridge by Esquire Hall's Old Mill and by Dr. Wakeman's in to the main road, and from the said Levell Bridge to the main road below Edward Hall's plantation, and from Dr. Middlemore's Cranberry Quarter to Mr. Aquilla Paca's, and to make good on half of the Levell Bridge - November, 1734.

LUKE STANSBURY appointed overseer of roads in Bush River Lower Hundred - November, 1734.

WILLIAM SAVORY appointed overseer of roads in the room of Benjamin Cadle in Gunpowder Neck - November, 1734.

CHRISTOPHER GIST appointed overseer of roads in the room of Samuel Owings - November, 1734.

PETER CARROL appointed overseer of roads in the room of Alexander Maccomus - November, 1734.

WILLIAM PETICOAT continued overseer of all the roads in Soldier's Delight Hundred lying between the Main Falls and Gwin's Falls of Patapsco, vizt., "the rowling road from Capt. Jones' Quarter, the road called the Indian Road from the Main Falls to Gwin's Falls, the rowling road from William Hamilton's to Dogwood Run, from the said Hamilton's unto the said Indian Road the directest way towards Court from the said Intion Road where it crosses such Level Branch to Mr. Gist's Mill." - November, 1734.

OLIVER CROMWELL appointed overseer of all the roads in the Patapsco Upper Hundred between the Main Falls and Gwin's Falls, vizt., "the roaling road from the Iron Works until it intersects the Indian Road, the roaling road from the head of Patapsco to the Dogwood Branch, the road from the Widow Teale's to John Mole's, from Mole's to the Lower Fording Place of Gwin's Falls, from William Hammond's to the Iron Works, the road from the Wading Place of Gwin's Falls to the Wading Place of the Main Falls of Patapsco, the road that leads from the Main Falls of Patapsco to Ragland Roaling Road, the road from the Main Falls of Patapsco to Mole's, the road from Ragland to Gwin's Falls where Charles Wells did live." - November, 1734.

EDWARD THORPE appointed overseer of roads in the room of Richard Wells from Col. Holland's Quarter to Dr. Wakeman's and also the road that leads from Robert West's to William Perkins' - November, 1734.

SKIPWITH COALE appointed overseer of roads from Rock Run to the ford and from Rock Run to Zachariah Spencer's - November, 1734.

SAMUEL STANSBURY appointed overseer of the highways in the room of John Rogers - November, 1734.

CHRISTOPHER RANDALL, JR. appointed overseer of the highways in Patapsco Upper Hundred in the room of Charles Wells - November, 1734.

WILLIAM LOWE appointed overseer of roads that lead from the Little Falls to Darby Henley's, from the Long Calm to the Little Falls, from Pickett's Landing Place to Nicholas Day's, and from Thomas Johnson's to Luke Stansbury's Mill - November, 1734.

THOMAS FRANKLIN appointed overseer of roads that lead from Darby Henley's to Nicholas Hutchins' and from thence to Luke Stansbury's Mill, and from thence to the most convenient place in "My Lady Baltimore's Manner" - November, 1734.

THOMAS SLIGH, on his own petition, is allowed to clear the following road at his own expence by the direction of Mr. Thomas Sheredine, vizt., "from the Widow Whitehead's to Patapsco Church along by George Harryman's and so to Thomas Broad's, and so to the Quaker Meetinghouse." - November, 1734.

THOMAS CRISSAP appointed overseer to clear a road from Connajohala to the Rock Run, and it is ordered that the inhabitants of Deer Creek assist in clearing the said road - November, 1734.

THOMAS TODD appointed overseer of roads from said Todd's house to the Herring Run and to Corbin's Run, and to have all the people from Corbin's Run down the neck to the Bayside and likewise all the people between Back River and the said road up to the Herring Run - November, 1734.

JOHN BOWEN, JR. appointed overseer of roads that lead from Corbin's Run to Jonathan's Mill, from thence to the Herring Run and from thence down to the old church, to make bridges and causeways and to take all the people in that precinct to clear the said road - November, 1734.

ZACCHEUS BARRET ONION continued overseer of road in 1762.

HUGH RAY continued overseer of road in 1762.

RICHARD WELLS, JR. continued overseer of road in 1762.

EDWARD DORSEY continued overseer of road in 1762.

WILLIAM MCCUBBIN appointed instead of John Addison Smith to oversee road from Herring Run to the north side of Northeast Run, from "TL" Road to the lower side of Northeast Creek at the Lancashire Works, and from Herring Run to where Patapsco Neck Road leading to Baltimore Town intersects the Main Road - 1762.

ISAAC RISTEAU continued overseer of road in 1762.

ASAEL GITTINGS continued overseer of road in 1762.

JOHN DEMMIT appointed instead of Absalom Butler to oversee road from Widow Butler's to Baltimore Town Gateway and from Baltimore Town Church until it intersects the road below William Lux's, and from Baltimore Town to the falls at Jonathan Hanson's old mill - 1762.

WALTER TOLLEY continued overseer of road in 1762.

RICHARD DAVIS appointed instead of John Reister to oversee road from Josephus Murray's to St. Thomas Church, and from there to Worthington's Mill and Pipe Creek Road from the Great Falls of the Patapsco where it crosses by Thomas Mathews' to the Conowangoe Wagon Road - 1762.

JOHN BELT, JR. appointed instead of Jeremiah Johnson to oversee road from Worthington's Mill across the great Conowago Road just below Josephus Murray's towards the Pipe Creek settlement - 1762.

BENJAMIN WAGERS appointed instead of Robert Tevis to oversee road from the Delaware Bottom to Digg's wagon road, then down the road to the Great Falls of the Patapsco - 1762.

JOHN CROSS, SR. continued overseer of road in 1762.

JOHN SCHOOLFIELD appointed instead of Henry Cross, Jr. to oversee road from Christopher Cole's by Dennis Cole's to Stephen Price's and then to John Price's, and from Stephen Price's to Absalom Barney's - 1762.

WILLIAM COLE (OF BUTLER RIDGE) appointed instead of Benjamin Bowen to oversee road from Baltimore Town by Benjamin Bowen's until it intersects the Court Road, from Baltimore Town by Joseph Taylor's until it intersects the Court Road, and from Hitcock's old field toward William Parrish's until it intersects the Court Road - 1762.

WILLIAM HORTON appointed instead of Michael Gilbert, Jr. to oversee road from the Thicket Plantation to the main road by Col. Hall's Quarters, from old Gervis Gilbert's place to Howell's Mill, and from the Thicket Plantation to the main road where Doctor Wakeman formerly lived, and on Church Road from Cowen's old place to Obediah Pritchard's old place, and of Quaker Road from Horner's place until it intersects the road from Cox's Mill to Bush Town - 1762.

HENRY YOUNG continued overseer of road in 1762.

THOMAS MILLER appointed instead of William Wilson to oversee road from Cox's Mill until it intersects the road from Rock Run by John Lyall's old fence, and from said mill to Farmer's Ford in Deer Creek - 1762.

WILLIAM BOZLEY continued overseer of road in 1762.

RICHARD RICHARDS continued overseer of road in 1762.

WILLIAM MURPHY appointed instead of John Hamilton to oversee road from William Hamilton, Sr.'s to Gwyn's Falls, from said Hamilton's by Ayer's Mill to Emanuel Teal's and from Widow Owings' to the Dead Run - 1762.

JOSEPH PRESBURY appointed instead of William Debrular to oversee road from Winter's Run down Gunpowder Neck to the lane between John Day's and William Hill's plantation as it formerly went to William Hills from Winter's Run to Jo. Buckley's and from Joppa until it intersects the road from Winter's Run to said lane, and from Bush River Ferry Place until it intersects the Gunpowder Neck Road on its way to Joppa - 1762.

ANDREW BUCHANAN continued overseer of road in 1762.

WILLIAM ASHMORE continued overseer of road in 1762.

JACOB GILES appointed instead of Luke Griffith to oversee road from the Susquehannah to Humphry's Run - 1762.

WILLIAM PARRISH continued overseer of road in 1762.

JAMES MATHERS [MATHEWS?] appointed instead of William Kitely to oversee road from the fork of the road at Thomas Bond's to Otter Point, and from Winter's Run to Binam's Run, and from Bynam's Run by the meeting house to Otter Point - 1762.

THOMAS WHEELER continued overseer of road in 1762.

JACOB DAVIS appointed instead of Col. William Young to oversee road from the Long Calm to Onion's Works, from thence to Mr. Dean's Run, and from thence by Col. Young's to the Long Calm - 1762.

JOSHUA BOND continued overseer of road from Thomas Bond's to Bull's Mill, and from Thomas Bond's to the fork of the road by Beaver Paine's, and from Jacob Bull's Mill to the great road near Samuel Durham's - 1762.

GEORGE OGG, JR. continued overseer of road in 1762.

JOHN SHERMANDINE appointed overseer of road from Widow Butler's to St. Thomas Church, from thence to North Run, and from said church to Gwin's Falls and from Dr. Lyons' Quarters where John Metcalf lived to Gwin's Falls, and from Thomas Bond's by Thomas Johnson's to Gwin's Falls - 1762.

RENALDO MONK appointed instead of George Risteau to oversee road from Samuwl Owings' until it intersects the main wagon road by Widow Butler's and from Thomas Bond's to Jones Falls, and from Monk's until it intersects the wagon road to Baltimore Town near Widow Buchanan's - 1762.

CHARLES CROXALL continued overseer of road in 1762.

COL. BENJAMIN YOUNG continued overseer of road in 1762.

JACOB COLLYDAY continued overseer of road in 1762.

RICHARD JACKS appointed instead of John Cook, Sr. to oversee road from Pontany's Mill to Evin Jones' and from thence to Shipley's Mill, then from the great road by Peter Gosnell's through John Clark's and so to St. Thomas Church - 1762.

EDWARD THARP appointed instead of John Bond (of Bush) to oversee road from Jerusalem to Widow Talbot's, and from Edward Thorp's to Bull's Mill, and from the Little Falls by John Bond's until it intersects the first mentioned road - 1762.

JOHN ANDERSON appointed instead of John Hughs to oversee road from Beaver Paine's to Benjamin Norris' quarters - 1762.

SAMUEL LEE continued overseer of road in 1762.

JOHN HARRIS appointed instead of Corbin Lee to oversee road from Johnson's Ford on Deer Creek to Antill Deaver's, and from Cox's Mill to John Chritard's, and from Lawrance Clark's to the Thickett Plantation - 1762.

REUBIN PERKINS continued overseer of road in 1762.

JOHN HALL (OF CRANBERRY) continued overseer of road in 1762.

JOHN WEBSTER appointed instead of James Webster to oversee road from Humphrey's Run to Bynam's Run and from his place to Bush Town - 1762.

SAMUEL GRIFFIN appointed instead of John Mathews to oversee road from Rumney Bridge to Level Bridge and from thence until it intersects said road - 1762.

JAMES TAYLOR continued overseer of road in 1762.

WILLIAM HOPKINS continued overseer of road in 1762.

PHILIP COLE appointed instead of Skipwith Cole to oversee road from Samuel Wallace's Bridge to Rock Run Warehouse - 1762.

JAMES LEE, SR. continued overseer of road in 1762.

JERVIS BIDDISON continued overseer of road in 1762.

WILLIAM ANDREW continued overseer of road from the head of Middle River where Jere. Biddison ends, round said river to where Daniel Scott lived, from the head of said river to County Road at the west end of Mr. Lawson's plantation, and from the place where Daniel Scott lived up to the County Road by Lawson's Furnace, and from Neck Gate near Pea Hill to the head of Salt Petre Creek - 1762.

THOMAS BIDDISON appointed instead of John Buck to oversee road from Northeast Run to the little valley at north end of Hatchman's house - 1762.

THOMAS TODD continued overseer of road in 1762.

HIGH SOLLERS appointed overseer of road from the run by Widow Gorsuch's plantation until it intersects the road leading from Herring Run down Patapsco Neck - 1762.

BRIAN PHILPOT apppointed overseer of road from the run from Widow Gorsuch's plantation to Baltimore Town, and from falls at Moore's Mill until it intersects aforesaid road, from west end of causey at Philpot's new bridge over said causey and bridge into Front Street, and of all streets and lands in that part of Baltimore Town, and the addition thereto on east side of Jones Falls - 1762.

THOMAS STANSBURY, JR. continued overseer of road in 1762.

LOVELESS GORSUCH continued overseer of road in 1762.

WILLIAM WILSON appointed overseer of road from Cox's Mill to James Run - 1762.

WILLIAM AMOS continued overseer of road in 1762.

GEORGE BOTTS continued overseer of road in 1762.

WILLIAM SMITH continued overseer of road in 1762.

ABSALOM BARNEY continued overseer of road in 1762.

MORRIS BAKER continued overseer of road in 1762.

JOSEPH NORRIS, SR. continued overseer of road in 1762.

WILLIAM SLADE appointed instead of Abraham Rutlage to oversee road from Mr. Boyce's to Charlott Town and from Boyce's to the place where George Eliott did live, and from Josias Slade's to where John Parker lived by the Little Falls, and from the wagon road from the Great Falls along by Widow Shepperd's until it intersects the wagon road from York to Joppa - 1762.

WILLIAM GRAFTON continued overseer of road in 1762.

HENRY CROSS continued overseer of road in 1762.

MORDECAI PRICE (SON OF MORDECAI) appointed instead of Thomas Sheredine to oversee road from Wheeler's Mill to Jo. Bozley's, and from Wheeler's Mill to Uriah Davis', and from said mill along the wagon road towards the manor to the Great Falls of the Gunpowder- 1762.

THOMAS MILES continued overseer of road in 1762.

JOHN WILMOT appointed instead of Neal Haile to oversee road from Stephen Price's to the Court Road and from Wheeler's Mill to the Court Road, and from John Daughaday's along by John Chilcoat's, William Gorsuch's, and the place that was formerly Charles Robinson's by Thomas Tipton, Jr.'s and Widow Carr's into the main road that leads to Baltimore Town - 1762.

ZACCHEUS BARRET ONION continued overseer of road in 1763.

HUGH RAY continued overseer of road in 1763.

JOSEPH MORGAN appointed instead of Richard Wells, Jr. to oversee road from Morgan's Mill to the great road to Rock Run and of the road from Bald Friar's Ferry leading to the chappell until it intersects the main road leading from Ashmore's Mill to Rock Run landing - 1763.

EDWARD DORSEY continued overseer of road in 1763.

FRANCIS PHILLIPS appointed instead of William McCubbin to oversee road from Perring Run to the north side of Northeast Run, from "TL" Road to the lower side of Northeast Creek at the Lancashire Works, and from Perring Run to where the Patapsco Neck Road leading to Baltimore Town intersects the Main Road - 1763.

ISAAC RISTEAU continued overseer of road in 1763.

ASAEL GITTINGS appointed (and continued) overseer of road from Roger Boyce's to the run by Mr. Dean's from Luke Stansbury's old mill place at the Great Falls by Charles Baker's to the Little Falls, and from Thomas Johnson's to Mr. Tolley's quarters, and from near D. Lynch's to the mill that formerly belonged to George Brown - 1763.

JOHN DEMMIT continued overseer of road in 1763.

CORBIN LEE appointed instead of Walter Tolley to oversee road from the Gunpowder Ferry to the little valley at the north end of the lane at Mr. Lawson's Works by Hatchman's old house, from the Great Falls of the Gunpowder until it intersects the county road by Roderick Cheyne's, and from the Great Falls along the Court Road opposite to Heathcote Picket's house - 1763.

BENJAMIN BOND appointed instead of Richard Davis to oversee road from Josephus Murray's to St. Thomas Church, and from there to Worthington's Mill and Pipe Creek Road from the Great Falls of the Patapsco where it crosses by Thomas Mathews' to the Conowangoe Wagon Road - 1763.

JOHN BELT, JR. continued overseer of road in 1763.

BENJAMIN WAGERS continued overseer of road in 1763.
JOHN CROSS, SR. continued overseer of road in 1763.
JOHN SCHOLFIELD continued overseer of road in 1763.
JOB EVANS appointed instead of William Cole (of Brittain Ridge) to oversee road from Baltimore Town by Benjamin Bowen's until it intersects the Court Road, from Baltimore Town by Joseph Taylor's until it intersects the Court Road, and from Hitcock's old field toward William Parrish's until it intersects the Court Road - 1763.
WILLIAM HORTON continued overseer of road in 1763.
HENRY YOUNG continued overseer of road in 1763.
THOMAS MILLER continued overseer of road in 1763.
WILLIAM BOZLEY continued overseer of road in 1763.
MICHAEL FISHER appointed instead of Richard Richards to oversee the road from Josephus Murray's to the temporary line - 1763.
NATHANIEL STINCECOMB appointed instead of William Murphey to oversee road from William Hamilton, Sr.'s to Gwyn's Falls, from said Hamilton's by Ayer's Mill to Emanuel Teal's, and from Widow Owings' to the Dead Run - 1763.
WILLIAM PRESBURY, SR. appointed instead of Joseph Presbury to oversee road from Winter's Run down Gunpowder Neck to the lane between John Day's and William Hill's plantation as it formerly went to William Hill's from Winter's Run to Jo. Buckley's, and from Joppa until it intersects the road from Winter's Run to said lane, and from Bush River Ferry Place until it intersects Gunpowder Neck Road on its way to Joppa - 1763.
WILLIAM BUCHANAN appointed instead of Andrew Buchanan to oversee road from the foot of Baltimore Town Bridge to Carroll's Mill, from Fell's Mill until it intersects aforesaid road, and from Baltimore Town to Ferry Point, and from Baltimore Forge to Baltimore Town - 1763.
WILLIAM ASHMORE continued overseer of road in 1763.
JACOB GILES continued overseer of road in 1763.
WILLIAM PARRISH continued overseer of road in 1763.
THOMAS BOND, SR. appointed instead of James Mathers to oversee road from the fork of the road at Thomas Bond's to Otter Point, and from Winter's Run to Binam's Run and from Bynam's Run by the meetinghouse to Otter Point - 1763.
THOMAS WHEELER continued overseer of road in 1763.
JONATHAN STARKEY appointed instead of Jacob Davis to oversee road from the Long Calm to Onion's Works, from thence to Mr. Dean's Run, and from thence to Col. Young's to the Long Calm - 1763.

JOSHUA BOND continued overseer of road in 1763.

GEORGE OGG, JR. continued overseer of road in 1763.

CORNELIUS HOWARD appointed instead of John Shammedine to oversee road from Widow Butler's to St. Thomas Church, from thence to North Run, and from said church to Gwin's Falls, and from Dr. Lyon's Quarters where John Metcalf lived to Gwin's Falls, and from Thomas Bond's by Thomas Johnson's to Gwin's Falls - 1763.

RENALDO MONK continued overseer of road in 1763.

CHARLES CROXALL continued overseer of road in 1763.

COL. BENJAMIN YOUNG continued overseer of road in 1763.

ALEXANDER WELLS appointed instead of Jacob Collyday to oversee road from Gwin's Falls to the fork of the roads by Evin Jones', and from thence down the wagon road to Widow Owings', and from the falls by Igo's to Church Road, and until it intersects the Great Road that leads from Mr. Hambleton's, and from the Great Road by Hammond's Quarters to Turnbull's Mill - 1763.

PETER GOSNELL appointed instead of Richard Jacks to oversee road from Pontany's Mill to Evin Jones', and from thence to Shipley's Mill, and then from the great road by Peter Gosnell's through John Clark's and so to St. Thomas Church - 1763.

EDMUND TALBOTT appointed instead of Edward Tharp to oversee road from Jerusalem to Widow Talbot's and from Edward Thorp's to Bull's Mill, and from the Little Falls by John Bond's until it intersects the first mentioned road - 1763.

ADAM MCGAW appointed instead of John Anderson to oversee road from Beaver Paine's to Benjamin Norris' quarters - 1763.

LAWRANCE CLARK appointed instead of Samuel Lee to oversee road from Capt. Paca's quarters to John Webster's - 1763.

RALPH SMITH appointed instead of John Harris to oversee road from Johnson's Ford on Deer Creek to Antill Deaver's, and from Cox's Mill to John Chritard's, and from Lawrence Clark's to the Thickett Plantation - 1763.

ARTHUR INGRAM appointed instead of Reubin Perkins to oversee road from Durbin's old plantation to Lower Ferry and from John Lyall's to Rock Run Warehouse - 1763.

JOHN HALL (OF CRANBERRY) continued overseer of road in 1763.

JOHN WEBSTER continued overseer of road in 1763.

SAMUEL GRIFFIN continued overseer of road in 1763.

JAMES TAYLOR continued overseer of road in 1763.

PHILIP COLE continued overseer of road in 1763.

JAMES LEE, SR. continued overseer of road in 1763.

JERVIS BIDDISON continued overseer of road in 1763.

WILLIAM ANDREW continued overseer of same road, plus the road from the head of Salt Petre to a gate below Nathan Nickols' house until it intersects the road by Lawson's Iron Works - 1763.

JOHN BUCK appointed instead of Thomas Biddison to oversee road from Northeast Run to the little valley at the north end of Hatchman's house - 1763.

THOMAS TODD continued overseer of road in 1763.

HIGH SOLLARS continued overseer of road in 1763.

BRIAN PHILPOTT continued overseer of road in 1763.

THOMAS STANSBURY, JR. continued overseer of road in 1763.

LOVELESS GORSUCH continued overseer of road in 1763.

WILLIAM WILSON continued overseer of road in 1763.

WILLIAM AMOS continued overseer of road in 1763.

JAMES PRITCHARD appointed instead of George Botts to oversee road from Thomas Kelly's by said Pritchard's to Rock Run Warehouse - 1763.

WILLIAM SMITH appointed (and continued) overseer of road from the fork of the road by Peter Whittacre's to Edward Thorp's and Winter's Run where John Denbo lived, and to the western fork of said run where John Chalk lives - 1763.

ABSALOM BARNEY continued overseer of road in 1763.

ISAAC DAWS appointed instead of Morris Baker to oversee road from Joppa to Bull's Run - 1763.

JOSEPH NORRIS, SR. continued overseer of road in 1763.

THOMAS TALBOTT appointed instead of William Slade to oversee road from Mr. Boyce's to Charlott Town and from Boyce's plantation where George Ellet lately lived, from Josias Slade's to the Little Falls along the wagon road from the Great Falls along by Widow Shepherd's until it intersects the wagon road from York to Joppa - 1763.

WILLIAM GRAFTON continued overseer of road in 1763.

HENRY CROSS continued overseer of road from Joseph Buckley's to the Great Falls of the Gunpowder - 1763.

MORDECAI PRICE (SON OF MORDECAI) continued overseer of road in 1763.

THOMAS BOND (SON OF THOMAS BOND OF BUSH) appointed instead of Thomas Miles to oversee road from the Little Falls by John Parker's to Widow Talbott's, and from thence by the York Wagon Road until it intersects the road from York to Bush River - 1763.

THOMAS RENSHAW appointed overseer of new road as lately laid out from his fence to John Horward's Mill - 1763.

EDWARD BULL appointed overseer of new road lately laid out from Robert Brierly's to John Horward's Mill, and from there to a place on Deer Creek called Bald Hill, and from said mill by Henry Green's door to where Stephen Rigdon formerly lived - 1763.

[Records on Overseers of Roads for 1764 are not extant.]

HENRY DAVIS appointed instead of John Greniff Howard to oversee road from Buckley's to Joppa Warehouse to the Little Falls at the Works and to Norris' old field until it intersects the main road from Joppa to the head of Bush River - 1765-1766.

HENRY BENNENTON continued overseer of road from the temporary line to Joseph Morgan's Mill - 1765-1766.

THOMAS NISBETT continued overseer of road from Joseph Morgan's Mill to the Great Road to Rock Run, and of the road from Bald Friar's Ferry Landing to the chappell until it intersects the main road leading from Ashmore's Mill to Rock Run Landing - 1765-1766.

EDWARD DORSEY continued overseer of road in 1765-1766.

WILLIAM FOWLER appointed instead of William Hick to oversee road from Herring Run to the north side of Northeast Run, from "TL" Road to the lower side of Northeast Creek at the Lancashire Works, and from Herring Run to where Patapsco Neck Road leading to Baltimore Town intersects the main road - 1765-1766.

WILLIAM QUINE appointed instead of Levin Roberts to oversee the Court Road from Heathcote Picket's to William Pierce's, from Stansbury's old mill place on the Great Falls of the Gunpowder until it intersects aforesaid road by the Piney Swamp, and to Herring Run where Valentine Larsh is building a mill, and from said old mill place to Joseph Sutton's until it intersects the Court Road leading to the Long Calm - 1765-1766.

ASAEL GITTINGS continued overseer of road in 1765-1766.

SAMUEL MERRYMAN continued overseer of road from Widow Butler's to Baltimore Town Gateway, and from Baltimore Town Church until it intersects the road below William Lux's, and from Baltimore Town to the falls at Jonathan Hanson's old mill - 1765-1766.

BENJAMIN BOND continued overseer of road in 1765-1766.

CORBIN LEE continued overseer of road in 1765-1766.

JOHN BELT continued overseer of road in 1765-1766.

JOHN BROWN (SON OF ABEL) appointed instead of Benjamin Burgess Chaney to oversee road from the Delaware Bottom to Diggs' wagon road and then down the road to the Great Falls of the Patapsco - 1765-1766.

HENRY CROSS, SR. continued overseer of road in 1765-1766.

JOHN SCHOLFIELD continued overseer of road in 1765-1766.

SAMUEL WHEELER continued overseer of road from Baltimore Town by Benjamin Bowen's until it intersects the Court Road, from Baltimore Town by Joseph Taylor's until it intersects the Court Road, and from Hitcock's old field toward William Parrish's until it intersects the Court Road - 1765-1766.

WILLIAM HORTON continued overseer of road in 1765-1766.

HENRY STUMP appointed instead of William Cox to oversee road in 1765-1766.

HENRY YOUNG continued overseer of road in 1765-1766.

WILLIAM BOSLEY continued overseer of road in 1765-1766.

JACOB OATES appointed instead of Michael Fisher to oversee road in 1765-1766.

NATHANIEL STINCECOMB continued overseer of road in 1765-1766.

JOHN BROWN appointed overseer of road from the lane by Joppa down Gunpowder Neck to the end of lane between John Day's and the Widow Hill's - 1765-1766.

JOSEPH PRESBURY appointed overseer of road from Winter's Run by Joseph Buckley's and from said run down Gunpowder Neck until it intersects the main road down the neck, and from Bush River until it intersects the main road by John Timmonds - 1765-1766.

BENJAMIN ROGERS continued overseer of road from the foot of Baltimore Town Bridge to Carroll's Mill, from Fell's Point until it intersects aforesaid road, and from Baltimore Town to Ferry Point, and from Baltimore Forge to Baltimore Town - 1765-1766.

WILLIAM ASHMORE continued overseer of road in 1765-1766.

SAMUEL HOWELL appointed instead of Jacob Giles to oversee road from the Susquehanna to Humphries Run - 1765-1766.

WILLIAM PARRISH continued overseer of road in 1765-1766.

AARON MCCOMAS appointed instead of Thomas Bond to oversee road from the Little Falls by John Parker's to Widow Talbott's and from thence by the York Wagon Road until it intersects the road from York to Bush River - 1765-1766.

IGNATIUS WHEELER continued overseer of road from Beaver Paine's to Deer Creek by Henry Green's Quarters, and from Benjamin Colegate's to William Bennett's Mill, and from George Rigdon's to Widow Scott's and from George Rigdon's to Lawrance Clark's - 1765-1766.

ROBERT FLEMING appointed instead of George Simmons to oversee road from the Long Calm to Onion's Works, from thence to Mr. Dean's Run, and from thence to Col. Young's to the Long Calm - 1765-1766.

JOSHUA BOND continued overseer of road in 1765-1766.
GEORGE OGG continued overseer of road in 1765-1766.
CORNELIUS HOWARD continued overseer of road in 1765-1766.
FRANCIS SOLLERS appointed instead of Renaldo Monk to oversee road from Samuel Owings' until it intersects the main wagon road by Widow Butler's and from Thomas Bond's to Jones Falls, and from Monk's until it intersects the wagon road to Baltimore Town near Widow Buchanan's - 1765-1766.
CHARLES CROXALL continued overseer of road in 1765-1766.
CAPT. JAMES CALDER appointed instead of Col. Benjamin Young to oversee road from Dead Run to Baltimore Forge Dam, from Baltimore Works to Hunting Ridge, and from John Penn's until it intersects the road from Patapsco Falls from Ragg Landing to Emanuel Teall's and of the road that is now used by carts, wagons and other carriages that leads through the lands called "Taylor's Forrest," "Pearce's Encouragement," and "Long Acres," to the ford over the main falls of Patapsco where the old road crosses - 1765-1766.
ALEXANDER WELLS continued overseer of road from Gwin's Falls to the fork of the roads by Evin Jones' and from thence down wagon road to Widow Owings', and from the falls by Igo's to Church Road, and until it intersects the Great Road that leads from Mr. Hambleton's, and from the Great Road by Hammond's quarters to Turnbull's Mill, and to clear the road as it has been laid out by Thomas Gist, Nicholas Orrick, and Christopher Carnan, according to a platt lodged here in court, from Alexander Wells' to Dr. Lyons' Gate - 1765-1766.
WILLIAM BOZEMAN appointed (and continued) overseer of road from Pontany's Mill to Evin Jones' and from thence to Shipley's Mill, and then from the great road by Peter Gosnell's through John Clark's and so to St. Thomas Church - 1765-1766.
PETER CARLISLE appointed to oversee road from Jerusalem to Widow Talbott's and from Edward Thorp's to Bull's Mill, and from the Little Falls by John Bond's until it intersects the first mentioned road - 1765-1766.
DAVID THOMAS appointed instead of Nicholas Boone to oversee road from Beaver Paine's to Benjamin Norris' Quarters - 1765-1766.
LAWRANCE CLARK continued overseer of road in 1765-1766.
THOMAS HARRISON appointed to oversee road from Johnson's Ford in Deer to Antill Deaver's, from Cox's Mill to John Chritard's, and from Lawrance Clark's to the Thickett Plantation - 1765-1766.
PHILIP GOVER appointed to oversee road from Durbin's old plantation to the Lower Ferry and from John Lyall's to the Rock Run Warehouse - 1765-1766.

JOHN HALL (OF CRANBERRY) continued overseer of roads as before, plus the road from the new bridge over the Cranberry until it intersects the road leading down to Long Bridge - 1765-1766.

JAMES OSBORN appointed instead of John Talbott to oversee road from Humphrey's Run to Bynam's Run and from John Webster's to Bush Town - 1765-1766.

SAMUEL GRIFFITH continued overseer of road in 1765-1766.

JAMES TAYLOR continued overseer of road in 1765-1766.

NATHAN RIGBIE continued overseer of road from Samuel Wallace's Bridge to Rock Run Warehouse - 1765-1766.

WILLIAM HOPKINS continued overseer of road from the chappell to the Quaker meeting house and from Ephraim Gover's to Farmer's Ford - 1765-1766.

ROBERT DUNN appointed to oversee road from Johnson's Ford to Samuel Webb's, and to William Bennett's Mill, and from the chapple until it intersects the Forrest Road by Thomas Johnson, Jr.'s - 1765-1766.

JARVIS BIDDISON continued overseer of road in 1765-1766.

WILLIAM ANDREW continued overseer of road in 1765-1766.

JOHN BUCK continued overseer of road in 1765-1766.

THOMAS TODD continued overseer of road in 1765-1766.

HIGH SOLLERS continued overseer of road in 1765-1766.

BRIAN PHILPOTT continued overseer of road in 1765-1766.

THOMAS STANSBURY, JR. continued overseer of road in 1765-1766.

LOVELESS GORSUCH continued overseer of road in 1765-1766.

WILLIAM WILSON continued overseer of road in 1765-1766.

WILLIAM AMOS continued overseer of road in 1765-1766.

JAMES PRITCHARD continued overseer of road in 1765-1766.

THOMAS SHARPE appointed instead of John Bowen to oversee road from the fork of the road by Peter Whittacre's to Edward Thorpe's, and Winter's Run where John Denbo lived, to the western fork of said run where John Chaulk lives - 1765-1766.

ABSALOM BARNEY continued overseer of road in 1765-1766.

JOHN TAYLOR appointed to oversee road from Joppa to Bull's Mill - 1765-1766.

JOSEPH NORRIS, SR. continued overseer of road in 1765-1766.

THOMAS TALBOTT continued overseer of road in 1765-1766.

BENJAMIN ANDERSON, JR. appointed overseer of road from the great road along Widow Shepherd's until it intersects the wagon road from York Town to Joppa at the Rock Stone - 1765-1766.

WILLIAM GRAFTON continued overseer of road in 1765-1766.

MORDECAI PRICE (SON OF MORDECAI) continued overseer of road in 1765-1766.

JOHN DAUGHERDY continued overseer of road from Stephen Price's to the Court Road and from Wheeler's Mill to the Court Road, and from John Daughaday's along by John Chilcoat's, William Gorsuch's, and the place that was formerly Charles Robinson's by Thomas Tipton, Jr.'s and Widow Carr's into the main road that leads to Baltimore Town - 1765-1766.

THOMAS BOND (SON OF THOMAS BOND OF BUSH) continued overseer of road in 1765-1766.

THOMAS RENSHAW continued overseer of road in 1765-1766.

EDWARD BULL continued overseer of road in 1765-1766.

THOMAS BAKER RIGDON continued overseer of road from Ashmore's Mill on Broad Creek to Ashmead's Mill on Deer Creek - 1765-1766.

[Records on Overseers of Roads for 1766 and 1767 are not extant.]

THOMAS ARCHER appointed in room of Isaac Webster to oversee public roads in Pertutia [Spesutia] Upper Hundred and from Bynam's Run to Humphrey's Run upon the Provincial Road - 1768-1769.

JOHN HALL (OF CRANBERRY) appointed in room of Samuel Griffin to oversee roads in Pertutia [Spesutia] Lower Hundred, and from Humphrey's Run to Swan Creek - 1768-1769.

REUBEN PERKINS continued overseer of public roads in Susquehanna Hundred and from Swan Creek to the Lower Ferry - 1768-1769.

CORBIN LEE continued overseer of road from the Long Calm to Herring Run by Kingsburry Works, and road below the road in Back River and Middle River Run - 1768-1769.

BENJAMIN INGRAM appointed "overseer of public roads above" - 1768-1769. [Note: No description was given, and earlier records are missing].

ASAEL GITTINGS appointed overseer of public roads in Gunpowder Upper Hundred from Roger Boyce's house to Benjamin Rogers' Mill and from Roger Boyce's to James Yoe's, and from Boyce's to the falls near Dulaney's quarters, and from said Boyce's to the falls by Widow Risteau's Mill - 1768-1769.

JOHN WILSON appointed overseer of public roads below Asael Gittings' precinct in the fork of the Gunpowder in Gunpowder Upper Hundred - 1768-1769.

JOHN HAWKINS continued overseer of public roads in Deer Creek Upper and Lower Hundreds, and of the road from Deer Creek to Rock Run - 1768-1769.

WILLIAM ROBINSON (Cryer) continued overseer of public roads in Bush River Lower Hundred, and from Winter's Run to Bynam's Run - 1768-1769.

FRANCIS PHILIPS appointed overseer of public roads in Baltimore Town East and Patapsco Lower Hundreds, except the road in Patapsco Neck that this court put under the care of another overseer, and also to clear a road as Mr. Plowman and Mr. Chamier think fit (if admitted by B. Rogers) - 1768-1769.

ZACHARIAH MACCUBBIN continued overseer of the road from Baltimore Town to the falls of Patapsco and to Hammond's Ferry and the Lower Ferry - 1768-1769.

SAMUEL COOKSON appointed overseer of road from his house to Baltimore Town and to the Great Falls of Patapsco at Puntney's Mill, from Joanna Miller's to the falls at Mrs. Hamilton's, and from Butler's to Old Court Road at Mr. Croxwell's [Cromwell's?] - 1768-1769.

SAMUEL OWINGS continued overseer of road from Cookson's to St. Thomas Church and from Dr. Lyons' store to his mill, and to the falls by Reasman's, from Samuel Owings' fence to Old Court Road at Mr. Cromwell's, from Peter Gozlin's to St. Thomas Church, and from Robinson's to St. Thomas Church - 1768-1769.

WILLIAM GIST appointed overseer of road from St. Thomas Church to Riston's - 1768-1769.

JOHN RISTON appointed overseer of road from his house to the main falls at Mathews' Mill and also to the entrance of the Barrance - 1768-1769.

GEORGE MYERS appointed overseer of road from where Riston ends to the provincial line - 1768-1769.

SAMUEL WORTHINGTON continued overseer of road from Stephen Gill, Jr.'s to Walter Smith's at the Court Road, from Worthington's Mill to St. Thomas Church, and from the Old Indian Road to Francis Wells' - 1768-1769.

BENJAMIN BOWEN appointed overseer of road from Fork Road by Richard Hopkins' to John Pitt's, and from thence to the road to Stephen Gill, Sr.'s - 1768-1769.

WILLIAM HARTIGIM appointed overseer of road from Christopher Sewell's to the Frederick County line - 1768-1769.

GEORGE OGG appointed overseer of road from Winchester Town to Mathews' Mill, and from his house to the falls - 1768-1769.

ARCHIBALD BUCHANAN appointed overseer of road from Zachariah Toulson's to Baltimore Town, and from Lash's Bridge to said town - 1768-1769.

NICHOLAS MERRYMAN (SON OF JOHN) appointed overseer of road from Wheeler's Mill up the main road leading to John Merryman, Sr.'s, and from thence to the Great Falls on the Gunpowder that leads to York County - 1768-1769.

JOHN FORSTER appointed overseer of road from the Great Falls on the Gunpowder to York County - 1768-1769.

DANIEL BOND appointed overseer of public roads in room of Abraham Garrett in Bush River Hundred, and also of the road now established as a public road from Deer Creek called McGumery's Ford until it intersects the road that leads from York Town to Bush River - 1768-1769.

JOSEPH NORRIS appointed overseer of road from Roger Boyce's to Josias Slade's, and from thence up to the province line and also from Josias Slade's to the Great Falls of the Gunpowder where Jacob Cox formerly lived, and also from Slade's to the Little Falls of the Gunpowder near John Carman's - 1768-1769.

EDWARD NORRIS (SON OF JOSEPH) appointed overseer of road from the main road by John Cox's at the head of the Little Falls of the Gunpowder by Sinclair's quarters and then by Joseph Norris' Sr.'s to Scott's Mill - 1768-1769.

JOHN BOND (OF FELLS POINT) "undertakes to have the road in good repair from Philpott's Bridge to Fell's Point for one thousand pounds of tobacco." - 1768-1769.

CHARLES GORSUCH (SON OF CHARLES) appointed overseer of road from Josias Slade's to Benjamin Rogers' Mill, and from thence to Ezekiel Towson's - 1768-1769.

JAMES MAXWELL continued overseer of road from Joppa to Bayside in Gunpowder Neck, from Joppa to Winter's Run, and from Winter's Run down Gunpowder Neck until it intersects the main road that goes down to said neck - 1768-1769.

THOMAS BOND appointed overseer of road from Winter's Run by Morris Baker's to Onion's Iron Works - 1768-1769.

THOMAS SOLLERS continued overseer of all roads in Patapsco Neck until they intersect the main road from Baltimore Town to the old courthouse at Joppa, "for which he is be allowed fifteen hundred pounds of tobacco." - 1768-1769.

NICHOLAS DORSEY, JR. appointed overseer of road from Christopher Sewell's to Puntney's Mill, and the Dillaway Bottom Road - 1768-1769.

DANIEL MCCOMAS (SON OF WILLIAM) appointed overseer of road from the Long Calm up to Bynam's Run by Onion's Works over the Mountain Run - 1768-1769.

[Records of Overseers of Roads in 1770-1771 are not extant].

It is certified that those persons that were taken to clear Thomas Brerewood, Esq.'s road are no ways exempt from clearing the other roads and being subject to respective overseers as if the said road had never been made - 1736.

SAMUEL WEBSTER appointed overseer of roads from Henry Garrett's to John Deavor's Landing, from the Widow Butterworth's to Thomas Shy's cross roads, from Roger Mathews' Quarters until it intersects the road that leads from Henry Garrett's to Deavor's Landing as aforesaid, from Michael Webster's to Binam's Run by William Bradford's and from John Webster's to James's Run that leads to the church, until some other person is appointed in his stead - June, 1737.

WILLIAM SMITH (Delph) appointed overseer of road from Rumney Bridge to Level Bridge and to make good one half of the said Level Bridge and from the church over the Long Bridge into the aforesaid road between the Old Church Bridge and Delph Bridge, and to take all the male taxables on the said road that are to the eastward of the road that leads from the church to James Phillips' between the head of Delph Creek and Rumney Creek until some other person is appointed in his stead - June, 1737.

JAMES PHILLIPS appointed overseer of road that leads from the main road at Humphry's Run down into Back River Neck and from the said road by Phillips' plantation to Rumney Bridge, and to make good the said Rumney Bridge, and to take all the male taxables at Aquila Hall's, Dr. Wakeman, and James Fowler, and also all the taxables in Bush River Neck and to the westward of the road that leads from the church into Bush River Neck - June, 1737.

AQUILA PACA appointed overseer of road from the Level Bridge through Aquila Hall's plantation to the church, and from said Level Bridge into the main road below Col. Edward Hall's plantation and from said Paca's house down by Dr. Middlemore's Cranberry Plantation and from thence across into the main road, and he is impowered to appoint any person to act in his stead - June, 1737.

WILLIAM SMITH continued overseer of road and to take all the taxables on said road that are eastward of the road that leads from the church to James Phillips' plantation between the head of Muskeeto Creek and Rumney Creek - August, 1737.

CAPT. AQUILA PACA continued overseer of road and to take all the taxable persons below the main road between John Hall, Esq.'s dwelling plantation and Swan Creek as low as the head of Muskeeto Creek - August, 1737.

JOHN FARMER appointed overseer of road from Robert West's old mill by the Widow Galloway's Quarter and down by John Cowen's into the great road from Thomas Shea's to the church until some other person is appointed in his stead - August, 1737.

ROBERT OWENS appointed overseer to clear the new road from Connawangoe down to Joseph Ellidge as Christopher Gist has marked it, until some other person is appointed in his stead - August, 1737.

NATHANIEL SHEPHARD appointed overseer of roads from the bridge on Charles' Run up to Michael Macnemara's Quarter - November, 1737.

GEORGE ASHMAN appointed overseer of road instead of John Wright - November, 1737.

CHARLES MERRYMAN appointed overseer of road instead of ....[blank] - November, 1737.

THOMAS SHEREDINE appointed to lay out a road from Hitchcock's Mill into the rolling road that goes down by Benjamin Bowen's Quarter as the old road used to go and that the same be cleared by the overseer of that precinct - March, 1737.

BENJAMIN PRICE appointed overseer of roads (in room of Mordecai Price) that leads from Mr. Brerewood's over the Great Falls of Gunpowder River and so down by Mordecai Price's until it intersects the Wolf Pit Bridge, and from said Brerewood's over Charles' Run and so along the Two Notched Road over the Great Falls to Teague Tracey's - November, 1738.

BENJAMIN JONES (Gunpowder Neck) appointed overseer (in room of William Dallam) of roads from Joppa Town to Acquila Massey's, from the three bridges until it intersects the main road by Price's Mill, and to take all the inhabitants below the Neck Road as also all the inhabitants below the three bridges to clear said road - November, 1738.

CAPT. SKIPWITH COALE appointed overseer of roads that Joseph Hopkins was overseer of last year, and he is impowered to appoint any person to act in his stead, which said roads to be cleared are all the public roads on the north side of Deer Creek - November, 1738.

ROBERT CHAPMAN, SR. appointed overseer of roads in the room of Richard Richardson - November, 1738.

THOMAS TIPTON appointed overseer of roads in the room of Joseph Beasman - November, 1738.

Ordered that the inhabitants on Susquahanah River between Broad Creek and Muddy Creek clear a road convenient for the "rowling their tobacco's" which road is to be laid out by Capt. Skipwith Coale and cleared at the expence of the said inhabitants - March, 1738.

THOMAS BOND, JR. appointed overseer of road and ordered to clear the road that goes to the Little Falls by Crockett's Quarter to the top of a hill next to the Little Falls - March, 1738.

NATH. SHEAPARD appointed overseer and ordered to clear the roads on the Mannor over the Little Falls leading to Crockett's Quarter to the top of a hill by said Quarter - March, 1738.

DR. CHARLES CARROLL has promised by his letter bearing date the 11th of February, 1738, directed to Mr. Gist, to clear a new main road from his mill race on Gwinn's Falls to the main road that leads from Baltimore Town to said falls at a small run near Mr. Charles Ridgeley's which said road said Carroll has promised to clear at his own expence and render the same passable sufficient both for man and horse according as the law in such cases directs. It is ordered therefore by this Court that when the said road is cleared as aforesaid that Mr. Thomas Sheredine and Mr. William Hammond view the same and if they find it cleared and crosswayed sufficient, that then it be taken and deemed the main road and that the other road be stopped up - March, 1738.

GEORGE STOKES appointed overseer of roads in the room of William Smith, deceased - March, 1738.

JAMES GARRETSON appointed overseer in the room of Peazley Ingram - March, 1740.

JOHN LLOYD appointed overseer of roads from Bynams Run to Joppa and from Joppa to the Little Falls of Gunpowder, and up the main road until it intersects the aforesaid main road to Joppa - March, 1740.

THOMAS COLE and WILLIAM DALLAM ordered to view the roads proposed by Mr. James Maxwell to be turned in Gunpowder Neck and which if they approve of Mr. Maxwell is to turn accordingly - March, 1740.

LORD PROPRIETARY agst. JOHN LLOYD - In this case John Lloyd was presented this Court for not repairing the Town Bridge tho' he was overseer thereof, whereupon the said John Lloyd appears and shewing sufficient reasons why he neglected the same, it is ordered by the court that the said presentment be struck off - March, 1740.

COL. NATHAN RIGBIE appointed overseer of roads in the room of Skipwith Coale - November, 1741.

JOHN LONG appointed overseer of road in the room of Walter Dallas - November, 1741.

DANIEL STANBURY appointed overseer of road in the room of Thomas Tipton - November, 1741.

DORSEY PETTICOATE appointed overseer of road in the room of John Hamilton - November, 1741.

JOHN BAILEY appointed overseer of road in the room of Emanuel Teal - November, 1741.

EDWARD STOCDALL appointed overseer of road in the room of Cornelius Howard - November, 1741.

BENJAMIN BOND appointed overseer of road in the room of John Lloyd - March, 1741.

PARKER HALL, by his own petition, is ordered to clear a road from his house to the main road from Deer Creek which goes through John Whiteacre's and Edward Wakeman's land, and that he keep it in repair at his own expence - March, 1741.

THOMAS BOND, SR., by his own petition, to have a road cleared through Thomas Richardson's plantation, it is referred to Mr. William Young and Mr. William Amos to lay it out as they think fit - March, 1741.

DARBY HERNLY, by his own petition, shows that whereas the main road that leads from the manner called "My Lady's Manner" to Joppa goes through this petitioner's plantation which is very disadvantageous to this petitioner, for which readn he hunbly prays to order the said road some other way which will be as convenient to the inhabitants and your petitioner will be duty bound to pray, it is ordered that William Standiford and William Young lay out the within road as they think proper - March, 1741.

WILLIAM PIKE appointed overseer of road in the room of David Thomas - March, 1741.

JOHN WILMOTT, JR. appointed overseer of road in the room of Samuel Hopkins - June, 1742.

Ordered that a "roaling road" be cleared from the plantation of Thomas Horner to Ford Barns' Landing or such other more convenient place on Susquahanah River, as RICHARD JOHNS (overseer of roads from said river to Humpgry's Run) shall lay out and direct, and that the aforesaid road for the future shall be kept in repair by the overseer of aforesaid road - June, 1742.

GREGORY FARMER appointed overseer of road in the room of Obediah Pritchard, and especially of the main road from Paca's Quarters up to West's Mill - June, 1742.

JOHN RATTENBURY appointed overseer of the roads in Patapsco Neck - June, 1742.

WILLIAM ANDREWS appointed overseer of road from Edward Day's to the extent of the parish, and from said Andrews' dwelling house to the road of Middle River - June, 1742.

JAMES TOLLEY appointed overseer of roads in the room of Walter Tolley - November, 1742.

SKELTON STANDIFORD appointed overseer of roads in the room of William Standiford - November, 1742.

PETER GOSNELL appointed overseer of roads in the room of Dorsey Petticoat - November, 1742.

ROBERT CLARK (Deer Creek) appointed overseer of roads in the room of James Preston and of the road from George Rigdon's to Abraham Boyd's - November, 1742.

NICHOLAS RUXTON GAY appointed overseer of roads in the room of Benjamin Bond - March, 1742.

WILLIAM ANDREWS, by his petition, ordered to have the road by his house go where he has made a line - March, 1742.

On the petition of the inhabitants of "My Lady's Mannor" to have a road cleared through said mannor to the main road that leads to the Town of Joppa, it is ordered that they clear it and keep it in repair at their own expence, and that said road be laid out by the present overseer - March, 1742.

The inhabitants of "My Lady's Mannor" exhibited to the Court the following petition: "Pray that an order be given for them to clear a road from the great wagon road on the back of said mannor through the mannor into the great rolling road that leads to Joppa and Patapsco for the said wagons as well as other of the back inhabitants to pass and repass they conserving it of great use and benefit as well for the said inhabitants, as all that lye contiguous and be a great encouragement to trade and commerce, and that an overseer may be appointed as your worships shall think fit." Accordingly granted and LUKE WILEY appointed overseer of said road - March, 1742.

On the petition of the inhabitants of the Fork of Gunpowder it is ordered that a road be cleared from Nicholas Hutchins' to Luke Stansbury's Mill and that the present overseer of them presents have the same laid out and cleared - June, 1743.

JOHN RENSHAW appointed overseer of roads from Renshaw's and Porter's Mill to Zachariah Spencer and from the mill to the Widow Bond's fields - August, 1743.

The inhabitants of Bush River Forrest petitioned the Court that "they were in great want of a road to be cleared from Skelton Standiford's to a meeting house by John Farmer's and from thence to Benjamin Colegate's which they are willing to clear at their own expence, but after it is cleared to be kept in repair by the overseers that is or shall hereafter be appointed" - August, 1743.

NATHANIEL RICHARDSON appointed overseer of roads in the room of Nicholas Ruxton Gay - November, 1743.

JONATHAN HANSON appointed overseer of roads in the room of John Merryman, Jr. - November, 1743.

REECE BOWEN appointed overseer of roads in the room of Daniel Stansbury - November, 1743.

THOMAS SPEIER appointed overseer of roads in the room of Mabry Helms - November, 1743.

Court ordered that a road be cleared from Patapsco Ferry through Baltimore Town over the New Bridge and through Jones Town until it intersects the old main road and that the overseer on each side of the falls shall make crossways, clear the roads and keep the bridge in good repair - November, 1743.

THOMAS FORD, JR. appointed overseer of roads in the room of John Willmott, Jr. - November, 1743.

RICHARD RUFF appointed overseer of roads in the room of Thomas Treadway - November, 1743.

THOMAS RICHARDSON appointed overseer of roads in the room of Thomas Bond, Jr. - November, 1743.

THOMAS RENSHAW and others, inhabitants of Deer Creek Forrest, petitioned the Court "over the necessity of a rolling road to be cleared from Samuel Brice's dwelling plantation to the rolling road that was formerly cleared by Zachariah Spencer's plantation." Accordingly granted and SAMUEL BRICE appointed overseer - November, 1743.

WILLIAM YOUNG petitioned to have the road cleared and kept in repair that goes from his house to Mr. Stephen Onion's Iron Works. The Court ordered that "the overseer of them adjacent presents have it accordingly done" - August, 1744.

JOHN HAMMILTON appointed overseer of roads in the room of Peter Gosnell - November, 1744.

THOMAS BOON appointed overseer of roads in the room of Thomas Speier - November, 1744.

JOHN PACA appointed overseer of roads in the room of Nath. Richardson - November, 1744.

JOHN METCALF appointed overseer of the highway in the room of Christopher Gist - November, 1744.

ISAAC WOOD appointed overseer of the highways in the room of Gregory Farmer - November, 1744.

DENNIS COLE appointed overseer of roads in the room of Thomas Ford, Jr. - November, 1744.

STEPHEN ONION made application to alter the neck road to Joppa at his own expence and it was granted - November, 1744.

JOHN PACA, HENRY GARRETT and JAMES LEE were ordered to clear a road from William Smith's Mill on Deer Creek into the main road to Treadaway's Landing and afterwards to be kept and maintained by the overseers of that precinct - November, 1744.

JOHN PEDDICOAT, CHRISTOPHER RANDALL and several others petitioned "to have a road cleared from the main road aginst Robinson's plantation the most convenient way to the church." Accordingly granted and JOHN HAMMILTON was appointed overseer and to clear from the main road aforesaid to Gwinn's Falls, and JOHN METCALF the present overseer from the falls aforesaid to the church - March, 1744.

WILLIAM GRAFTON appointed overseer of roads from the "roolinghouse" to Dr. Middlemore's Landing - March, 1744.

JONATHAN CHAPMAN on behalf of William Chitwynd, Esq., and Company, petitioned "for a road to a convenient landing on the northwest branch of Patapsco River." Accordingly granted at their own expence, with MAJOR THOMAS SHEREDINE appointed to inspect the same - March, 1744.

WILLIAM KNIGHT petitions with several others for an order of court for a road either through or round Dom: Bucklar Patridge, which was accordingly granted - June, 1745.

RICHARD ROBERTSON appointed overseer of roads in the room of John Tayler, deceased - August, 1745.

CHARLES WORTHINGTON appointed overseer of roads in the room of James Leigh - November, 1745.

MATTHEW BECK appointed overseer of roads in the room of James Maxwill - November, 1745.

NICHOLAS HAILE appointed overseer of roads in the room of John Wyley - November, 1745.

DANIEL PRESTON appointed overseer of roads from William Smith's Mill to the road by Ignatius Wheeler's gate where he use to begin through the said Wheeler's plantation wherer the road has usually gone, and likewise that he clear the road from David Thomas' plantation in to the other road as Capt. William Young and Mr. John Paca shall lay it out - November, 1745.

JAMES CAIN appointed overseer of roads from Deer Creek by Thomas Johnson's to James' Run and from Deer Creek by the Widow Jarman's to the intersection of the above roads, and the church road from Joseph Butterworth's to the intersection of the church road that leads from Deer Creek by Michael Gilbert's near James Gallion's old place - November, 1745.

SAMUEL WEBSTER is to clear the roads as usual and add to his warrant to clear the roads from John Paca's Quarter by Dear [Deer] Creek to the place he used to begin at - November, 1745.

HETHCOAT PICKETT appointed overseer of roads from John Campbell's to the Great Falls and from the falls until it intersects the ferry road, then from the free school until it intersects the ferry road towards Edward Day's and from the pines to the school house - November, 1745.

Court Memorandum: Middle River Hundred is to be divided with the road from Mr. Stansbury's old mill to the place he formerly lived - November, 1745.

NICHOLAS HAILE ordered to lay out the road from Wheeler's Mill to the church as convenient as he can and that the overseer or overseers for the future clear the same - March, 1745.

JOHN PACA, JR. appointed overseer of the roads his father kept - March, 1745.

ISAAC WEBSTER filed a petition for "the turning a road" and it was granted accordingly - March, 1745.

WILLIAM PARRISH, JR. appointed overseer of road from Wheeler's Mill to Josias Slade's - June, 1746.

JOHN RIDGELY appointed overseer of roads from Carroll's Mill to Butler's, from thence to the bridge in Baltimore Town, from said bridge to Patapsco Ferry, and from said bridge to Carroll's Mill - August, 1746.

WILLIAM SMITH appointed overseer of roads in the room of Samuel Webster, and it is ordered that the road that leads out of said road to the church shall be cleared by the said inhabitants until it intersects the main road - August, 1746.

JOHN BAILEY appointed overseer of road from Dead Run to Moale's Point, from thence to the Great Falls, and thence to Gwin's Falls, and from Moale's Point to Ayer's Mill - November, 1746.

JOHN METCALFE appointed overseer of road from Butler's up the wagon road to Gwin's Falls to Thomas Bond's court road and from Gwin's Falls to the church, and from thence to the North Run - November, 1746.

GEORGE ASHMAN appointed overseer of road from North Run to Butler's New Design, from Thomas Bond's to Jones Falls, and from James Welsh's to the main road - November, 1746.

WILLIAM BARNEY, Jr. appointed overseer of road from Baltimore Town to the Herring Run and from said town up Brittain Ridge "rooling road to Setter Hill" [rolling road to Satyr Hill] and up the other part of Brittain Ridge rolling road to Benjamin Bowen's, and also that part of the rolling road that leads to

Richard Stevenson's, and from Baltimore Town up the road by the meeting house to Joseph Taylor's - November, 1746.

LUKE TROTTEN appointed overseer of road from North Point up to the Herring Run and from said point to the county road, and from Herring Run to the place where the old church stood - November, 1746.

JOHN WILLMOTT, JR. appointed overseer of road from the "rooling road at Setter Hill" [rolling road at Satyr Hill] to the Western Run of Gunpowder, and from Gunpowder Falls until it intersects the rolling road and from Nicholas Haile's Mill to "Cammell's als. Roberts" plantation - November, 1746.

RICHARD BOND appointed overseer of road from Benjamin Bowen's to Stephen Gill's and from the rolling road that leads from Dennis Garrett Cole's to the meeting house to the North Run, and from Dennis Cole's to Setter Hill - November, 1746.

EDWARD STOKSDALL [STOCKSDALE] appointed overseer of road from Josephus Murray's Quarter over Gwin's Falls, and to maintain and keep the bridge in good repair - November, 1746.

JOHN HAMILTON appointed overseer of road from the main falls to the court road to Gwin's Falls, and to keep the bridge over the falls in good repair, and from William Hamilton's to Ben's Run and keep the bridge over the said run in good repair, and from Peter Gosnell's to the Dead Run and that part of the said road which leads to Ragland Rolling Road until it intersects the said road, and from Nicholas Dorsey's until it intersects Peter Gosnell's Rolling Road, and from Nathaniel Stinchcomb's to Gwin's Fall which leads to St. Thomas Church - November, 1746.

JAMES PRESTON appointed overseer of roads in the room of Daniel Preston - November, 1746.

CHARLES WORTHINGTON continued overseer of roads he was overseer of last year - November, 1746.

GEORGE BROWN (Joppa) appointed overseer of roads in the room of William Copeland - November, 1746.

JOHN CHAMBERLAIN appointed overseer of roads in the room of Thomas Hutchins - November, 1746.

JAMES SCOTT appointed overseer of roads from the road that leads from his house to the Widow Scott's, and the road from William Grafton's which intersects said road - November, 1746.

AQUILA SCOTT appointed overseer of roads from the Widow Scott's to Dr. Middlemore's Landing, and from Jacob Bull's Mill intersecting said road - November, 1746.

JAMES CAINE continued overseer of roads as he was last year - November, 1746.

ISAAC WOOD appointed overseer of roads between the main road which leads from Humphrey's Run to Suscohana [Susquehanna] and Deer Creek, except such part as are in James Caine's precinct - November, 1746.

WILLIAM SMITH appointed overseer of roads from Smith's Mill on Deer Creek as laid out down to Deavor's Landing from James Run by Michael Webster's into said road, and the church road from John Webster's into the main road and from the Rolling Road to Capt. Bradford's - November, 1746.

MATHEW BECK continued overseer of roads as last year - November, 1746.

THOMAS TREADWAY appointed overseer of roads from Bynam's Run to Humphry's Run - November, 1746.

GEORGE GARRETSON appointed overseer of roads from Suscohanah [Susquehanna] Ferry to Humphry's Run and the church road that leads out of said road to the church - November, 1746.

JOHN PACA, JR. continued overseer of roads as last year - November, 1746.

WILLIAM ANDREW continued overseer of roads as last year - November, 1746.

GEORGE PRESBURY continued overseer of roads as last year - November, 1746.

JAMES GARRETSON appointed overseer of roads from the church to the bottom of Bush River Neck, and from the church into the neck road and over the Long Bridge, and from Phillips' to the Levell Bridge - November, 1746.

HEATHCOT PICKETT continued overseer of roads as last year - November, 1746.

GEORGE HARRYMAN appointed overseer of roads from T. L., the road leading to the bottom of the neck, from Hopewell to the head of Middle River, and from the head of Middle River until it intersects the neck road - November, 1746.

[No court proceedings are available between 1747 and 1750.]

CORNELUS HOWARD and THOMAS GEST ordered to lay out a road from Samuel Owings' plantation where William Lewis lately dwelt in to the main wagon road to be cleared at said Owings' expence - August, 1750.

NATHAN BOWEN apointed overseer of road from Richard Hopkins' to William Worthington's Quarter until November next - August, 1750.

JOSEPH ARNOLD appointed overseer of roads in the room of Charles Pairpoint - November, 1750.

JOHN STINCHICOMB appointed overseer of roads in the room of John Randell - November, 1750.

WILLIAM ANDREWS appointed overseer of roads in the room of William Savory - November, 1750.

JOHN GILL appointed overseer of roads in the room of William Gist - November, 1750.

EDWARD PARRISH appointed overseer of roads in the room of Edward Stoxdill [Stocksdale] and to clear a road from Gwin's Falls at James Wells' to the church - November, 1750.

NICHOLAS ORRICK appointed overseer of roads in the room of Robert Gilgrist - November, 1750.

JERVIS GILBERT appointed overseer of roads in the room of Andrew Thompson - November, 1750.

MORRIS BAKER appointed overseer of roads in the room of Peter Carroll - November, 1750.

HENRY BEECH appointed overseer of roads in the room of Moses Ruth - November, 1750.

RICHARD WILMOTT appointed overseer of roads in the room of John Chamberlain - November, 1750.

EDWARD TALBOT appointed overseer of roads in the room of John Colegate - November, 1750.

JOHN HERRYMAN [HARRYMAN] appointed overseer of roads in the room of Tague Tracey - November, 1750.

JAMES BILLINGSLEY appointed overseer of roads in the room of William Rigdon - November, 1750.

JOHN LONG appointed overseer of roads from the bottom of Back River to North East Works and from thence to the head of Middle River and from the head of Middle River until it intersects the first mentioned road - November, 1750.

LYDE GOODWIN appointed overseer of roads in the room of Richard Croxall - November, 1750.

[No court proceedings are available between 1751 and 1754.]

The Court resolved that a good and complete bridge shall be built over the Little Falls at or near where the main road crosses by Onion's Works, that THOMAS FRANKLIN, WALTER TOLLEY, ROBERT ADAIR, ROGER BOYCE, WILLIAM SMITH or the major part of them to be are are authorized and empowered Commissioners to advertise, meet, agree and contract with the undertaker or undertakers for that purpose - August, 1754.

Whereas the bridge over Jones Falls at Baltimore Town is much damaged and made impassable by a late Fresh [sic], said bridge being built by Mr. John Ridgely as per contract lodged in Baltimore County Court appears. On motion whether or not said contract should be complied with the Court was divided as follows: T: Franklin, Cha: Ridgely, Roger Boyce and William Lyon that it ought not, and Samuel Owings, William Smith, Robert Adair and Walter Tolley that it should be complied with - August, 1754.

JOHN BOREING appointed overseer of roads in the room of Josephus Murray - November, 1754.

JOHN HAMILTON appointed overseer of roads from Baltimore Town by Benjamin Bowen's until it intersects the Court Road, from said town by Samuel Hopkins until it intersects the Court Road from said town, by Joseph Taylor's until it intersects the Court Road and from Hitchcock's old field toward William Parrish's until it intersects the Court Road - November, 1754.

GEORGE PRESBURY appointed overseer of roads from Winters Run to the bottom of Gunpowder Neck and from Winters Run to Joseph Buckley's and from Joppa until it intersects the road from Winters Run to the bottom of Gunpowder Neck - November, 1754.

CHRISTOPHER VAUGHAN appointed overseer of roads from Christopher Cole's by Dennis Cole's to Stephen Price's and from thence to John Price's and from Stephen Price's to Absalom Barney's - November, 1754.

SAMUEL DAY appointed overseer from Roger Boyce's to Charlott Town and from said Boyce's to the plantation where George Elliott did live and from Josiah Slade's to where John Parker lived by the Little Falls, and the wagon road from the Great Falls along by Widow Shepherd's until it intersects the wagon road from York to Joppa - November, 1754.

WILLIAM PONTENY appointed overeer of roads from the foot of Baltimore Town bridge - November, 1754.

THOMAS GITTINGS, JR. continued overseer of roads - November, 1754.

PATRICK MONTGOMERY continued overseer of roads - November, 1754.

BENJAMIN KIDD WILSON continued overseer of roads - November, 1754.

WILLIAM PARISH, JR. continued overseer of roads - November, 1754.

WILLIAM KITELY continued overseer of roads - November, 1754.

JOHN PILES continued overseer of roads - November, 1754.

HENRY GARRETT continued overseer of roads - November, 1754.

JOHN WOODEN, JR. continued overseer of roads - November, 1754.

JACOB BOND continued overseer of roads - November, 1754.

EDWARD NORRIS appointed overseer of road from Joppa to Bull's Mill - November, 1754.

THOMAS ELLIOTT continued overseer of roads - November, 1754.

GEORGE OGG, JR, continued overseer of roads - November, 1754.

JOHN SIMKINS continued overseers of roads - November, 1754.

JOSEPH CROWMELL continued overseer of roads - November, 1754.
DUTTON LANE continued overseer of roads - November, 1754.
CHARLES CROXALL continued overseer of roads - November, 1754.
MCLANE BAILEY continued overseer of roads - November, 1754.
NICHOLAS ORRICK continued overseer of roads - November, 1754.
BEALE BOND [? page torn] continued overseer of roads - November, 1754.
THOMAS BOND, JR. continued overseer of roads - November, 1754.
JOSEPH NORRIS continued overseer of roads - November, 1754.
RICHARD DEAVOR continued overseer of roads - November, 1754.
MOSES RUTH continued overseer of roads - November, 1754.
THOMAS THOMPSON continued overseer of roads - November, 1754.
POLLARD KEENE continued overseer of roads - November, 1754.
JNO. HAMPTON continued overseer of roads - November, 1754.
ISAAC WOOD continued overseer of roads - November, 1754.
RICHARD JOHNS continued overseer of roads - November, 1754.
JOHN HALL (OF CRANBERRY) continued overseer of roads - November, 1754.
ISAAC WEBSTER continued overseer of roads - November, 1754.
JOHN MATTHEWS continued overseer of roads - November, 1754.
JAMES TAYLOR continued overseer of roads - November, 1754.
WILLIAM HOPKINS continued overseer of roads - November, 1754.
EDWARD WARD continued overseer of roads - November, 1754.
WILLIAM BENNETT continued overseer of roads - November, 1754.
JERVIS BIDDISON continued overseer of roads - November, 1754.
WILLIAM ANDREW continued overseer of roads - November, 1754.
JOSEPH WATKINS continued overseer of roads - November, 1754.
JOHN SKINNER continued overseer of roads - November, 1754.
PHILIP JONES continued overseer of roads - November, 1754.
JOHN MOORE continued overseer of roads - November, 1754.
JONATHAN STARKEY continued overseer of roads - November, 1754.
WILLIAM TOWSON continued overseer of roads - November, 1754.
THOMAS STANSBURY, JR. continued overseer of roads - November, 1754.
LOVELESS GORSUCH continued overseer of roads - November, 1754.
JOHN BULL continued overseer of roads - November, 1754.
THOMAS DURBIN continued overseer of roads - November, 1754.
BENJAMIN AMOS continued overseer of roads - November, 1754.
ABSALOM BARNEY continued overseer of roads - November, 1754.

ROBERT TIERS continued overseer of roads - November, 1754. [Note: This is probably Robert Tivis, not Robert Tiers].

JNO. EVANS appointed overseer of Diggs Wagon Road from Nicholas Dorsey's to Frederick County - November, 1754.

JNO. MERRYMAN appointed overseer of roads - November, 1754.

RICHARD JOHNSON appointed to open and clear Old Quaker Road from William Perkin's Ferry to the intersection of the road leading from Durbin's old plantation to Susquehannah Lower Ferry - June, 1755.

ISAAC WOOD appointed to open clear Old Quaker Road from where the road from Durbin's old plantation to Susquehannah Lower Ferry crosses it by Thomas Horner's until it intersects the main road by John Critchet's - June, 1755.

THOMAS GITTINGS and BEN. KIDD WILSON appointed to view lay out of road by Mr. Tolley's plantation near Long Green that leads to the Great Falls by Luke Stansbury's old mill, and report to the County Court - June, 1755.

JOHN WEST appointed overseer of road from the lower part of Pennsylvania down to Joseph Morgain's Mill on Broad Creek, and from thence to the great road that leads to Rock Run - August, 1755.

WILLIAM JOHNSON appointed in room of Jos. Watkins to oversee the road from Perring River to northside of Northeast Run, from T. L. Road [sic] to lower side of Northeast Creek at the Lancashire Works, and from Perring Run to where Patapsco Neck Road leading to Baltimore Town intersects the Main Road - November, 1755.

JOSEPH LEWIS appointed in room of Thomas Gittings, Jr. to oversee road from Roger Boyce's to the run by Mr. Dean's from Luke Stansbury's old mill place at the Great Falls by Charles Baker's to the Little Falls, and from Thomas Johnson's to Mr. Tolley's Quarters - November, 1755. John Young above roads [sic].

EZEKIEL SLADE appointed in room of Samuel Day to oversee road from Mr. Boyce's to Charlott Town and from Boyce's to plantation where George Elliott did live, and from Josias Slade's to where John Parker lived by Little Falls, and from the wagon road from Great Falls along by the Widow Sheppard's until it intersects the wagon road from York to Joppa - November, 1755.

JAMES TALBOT appointed instead of Thomas Elliott to oversee road from Little Falls by John Parker's to Widow Talbot's, and from Widow Talbot's up the wagon road until it intersects the wagon road to Bush River - November, 1755. Thomas Miles, Jr., in his room [sic].

SAMUEL STANSBURY, SR. appointed instead of William ----, to oversee the Court Road from Heathcote Picket's to William Pearce's, from Stansbury's old mill place on the Great Falls of Gunpowder to Heathcote Picket's, and from the mill place until it intersects the Court Road to Isaac Risteau's late dwelling plantation - November, 1755. Joseph Sutton addition [sic].

JOHN DEMMIT appointed instead of John Wooden, Jr. to oversee road from Widow Butler's to Baltimore Town Gateway, and from Baltimore Town Church until it intersects William Lux's, and from Baltimore Town to the falls at Jonathan Hanson's old mill - November, 1755.

HEATHCOTE PICKET appointed instead of Jonathan Starkey to oversee road from Gunpowder Ferry to little valley at north end of lane at Mr. Lawson's Works by Hatchman's old house, from the Great Falls of the Gunpowder until it intersects the road by Roderick Cheyne's, and from the Great Falls along the Court Road up opposite to Heathcote Picket's house - November, 1755.

THOMAS MATHEWS appointed instead of Dutton Lane to oversee road from Josephus Murray's to St. Thomas Church, and from there to Worthington's Mill, and Pipe Creek Road from the Great Falls of the Patapsco where it crosses by Thomas Mathew's to the Conowangoe Wagon Road - November, 1755.

BENJAMIN WHIPS appointed instead of Robert Tivis [Tevis] to oversee road from Delaware Bottom to Diggs' wagon road, and then down the road to the Great Falls of Patapsco - November, 1755.

JOHN CROSS, SR. appointed instead of John Merryman to oversee road lately laid out by Mordecai Price and John Merryman from the temporary line until it intersects Rolling Road that comes by John Merryman's to Wheeler's Mill - November, 1755.

GEORGE ENSOR appointed instead of Christopher Vaughan to oversee road from Christopher Cole's by Dennis Cole's to Stephen Price's and then to John Price's, and from Stephen Price's to Absalom Barney's - November, 1755. Richard Vaughan appointed [sic].

SAMUEL HOPKINS appointed instead of Nicholas Merryman to oversee road from Baltimore Town by Benjamin Bowen's until it intersects the Court Road, from Baltimore Town by Joseph Taylor's until it intersects the Court Road, and from Hitcock's old field toward William Parrish's until it intersects the Court Road - November, 1755.

DANIEL DURBIN appointed instead of John Hampton to oversee road from Thicket plantation to the main road by Col. Hall's Quarters, from old Gervis Gilbert's place to Howell's Mill, and from Thicket Plantation to the main road where Doctor Wakeman formerly lived - November, 1755. Charles Gilbert appointed [sic].

HENRY YOUNG appointed instead of Thomas Thompson to oversee road from said Thompson's house to John Webster's - November, 1755.

ISAAC WOOD is continued as overseer of Quaker Road from where the road from Durbin's old plantation to Susquehannah Lower Ferry crosses it by Thomas Horner's until it intersects the road by John Critchet's, and "ordered the following persons or those who shall dwell within the distance, they now do assist in keeping said road in repair: Thomas Horner, Daniel Anderson, Robert West, James Love, Robert Madole, Daniel Rute, James McCabe, Ephraim Andrews, James Seal, James Archer, Isaac Martin, Alexander Ette [Etle?], John Martin, Henry Stump, William Mecin, Robert Mills, James Martin, Thomas Sanders, Isaac Wood, Jr., Benjamin Culver, Joseph Smith, Timothy Keen, Robert Jeffery, John Critchet, Thomas Kenneday, and Robert Thompson" - November, 1755. William Cox appointed [sic].

CORNELIUS BRADY appointed instead of Benkid Willson to oversee road from Roger Boyce's to Isaac Risteau's Mill, and from said Boyce's by Richard Wilmot's to falls by Samuel Meredeth's, and by Thomas Gittings and John Chamberlain's until it intersects the road from Thomas Johnson by Walter Tolley's qyarters as it was laid out by said Tolley and Ruxton Gay, and from said Boyce's to the Great Falls where Stansbury's old mill was - November, 1755. William Trapnell appointed [sic].

BENJAMIN POWELL appointed overseer of road from Stephen Price's to the Court Road, and to Wheeler's Mill to Court Road - November, 1755. Stephen Price appointed [sic].

JOHN BOREING apointed overseer of road from Josephus Murray's to the temporary line - November, 1755.

JOHN HAMILTON continued as overseer of road from William Hamilton, Sr.'s to Gwyn's Falls, from said Hamilton's by Ayer's Mill to Emmel Teal's, and from Widow Owings to the Dead Run - November, 1755.

THOMAS MITCHELL continued as overseer of road from the Susquehannah to Humphry's Run - November, 1755. Robert Patterson appointed [sic].

GEORGE PRESBURY continued as overseer of road from Winter's Run to bottom of Gunpowder Neck, and from Winter's Run to Joseph Buckle's [Buckley's], and from Joppa until it intersects the road from Winter's Run to bottom of Gunpowder Neck - November, 1755.

WILLIAM PONTENY continued as overseer of road from the foot of Baltimore Town Bridge to Carroll's Mill, from Fell's Mill until it intersects aforesaid road, and from Baltimore Town to Ferry Point, and from Baltimore Forge to Baltimore Town - November, 1755. Edward Lewis, Jr. appointed [sic].

PATRICK MONTGOMERY continued as overseer of road from Samuel Wallace's Bridge to the temporary line, and from said bridge to Ashmore's Mill - November, 1755.

WILLIAM PARRISH continued as overseer of road from Roger Boyce's to the Great Falls near William Rogers' plantation - November, 1755.

WILLIAM KITELY continued as overseer of road from the fork of road at Thomas Bond's to Otter Point, and from Winter's Run to Binam's Run, and from Bynam's Run by the meeting house to Otter Point - November, 1755. Alexander McComas, carpenter [sic].

THOMAS WHEELER appointed in room of John Piles to oversee road from Beaver Payn's to Deer Creek by Henry Green's Quarters, and from Benjamin Colegate's to William Bennett's Mill, and from George Rigdon's to Widow Scott's, and from George Rigdon's to Lawrance Clark's - November, 1755. Henry Green appointed [sic].

HENRY GARRETT appointed overseer of road from Long Calm to Onion's Works, from thence to Mr. Dean's Run, and from thence by Col. Young's to the Long Calm - November, 1755. Jacob Davis appointed [sic].

JACOB BOND appointed overseer of road from Thomas Bond's to Bull's Mill, and from Thomas Bond's to the fork of road by Beaver Pain's - November, 1755.

GEORGE OGG, JR. appointed overseer of road from his house to main falls of Patapsco, and from thence by Thomas Mathews' to Frederick County - November, 1755.

JOHN SIMPKINS appointed overseer of road from Widow Butler's to St. Thomas Church, and from thence to North Run, and from said church to Gwin's Falls and by Joseph Cromwell's and Cornelius Howard's, from Thomas Bond's to How's Mill, and from How's Mill to the wagon road above Widow Butler's - November, 1755.

JOSEPH CROMWELL appointed overseer of road from Samuel Owings until it intersects the main wagon road by Widow Butler's and from Thomas Bond's to Jones Falls, and from Monk's until it intersects the wagon road to Baltimore Town near Widow Buchanan's - November, 1755. November, 1756 - George Risteau in room of Joseph Cromwell [sic].

CHARLES CROXALL appointed overseer of road from head of the Patapsco to Dr. Carroll's Mill on Gwyn's Falls, from thence to Moale's Point, and from thence to head of the Patapsco - November, 1755.

MCLANE BAILY continued as overseer of road from Dead Run to Baltimore Forge dam, from Baltimore Works to Hunting Ridge and from John Penn's until it intersects road to Patapsco Falls, and from Ray Landing to Emmanuel Teal's - November, 1755.

NICHOLAS ORRICK continued as overseer of road from Widow Owings to Shipley's Mill, from where the Court Road crosses said road to the main falls of Patapsco, from the main falls by Joshua Sewell's plantation until it intersects said road, and from the eastside of Gwyn's Falls where John Simkins ends by Nicholas Orrick's until it intersects the main road by Jones' Quarters, and the church road, and from Gwyn's Falls until it intersects the great road that leads from William Hamilton's - November, 1755. Return of new road by Jos. Owings and N. Orrick [sic].

ISAAC RISTEAU appointed overseer of road from Little Falls to Joppa and from thence to Buckley's, and from Buckley's to the Falls again- November, 1755. Jos. Smith appointed [sic]. [Note: There is a large "X" through this entry in the minute book.]

JOSEPH NORRIS appointed overseer of road from Beaver Pain's to Benjamin Norris' Quarters - November, 1755.

THOMAS BOND, JR. appointed overseer of road from Jerusalem to Widow Talbot's, and from Edward Thorp's [Tharp's?] to Bull's Mill, and from Little Falls by John Bond's until it intersects the first mentioned road - November, 1755. Daniel Tredway appointed [sic].

RICHARD DEAVER appointed overseer of road from Deer Creek by his house to Thomas Crabtree's - November, 1755.

MOSES RUTH appointed overseer of road from Capt. Paca's Quarters to John Webster's - November, 1755.

POLLARD KEEN continued as overseer of road from Johnson's Ford on Deer Creek to Antill Deaver's, and from Cox's Mill to John Critchard's [Critchet's], and from Law. Clark's to Thickett Plantation to Benjamin Culver's - November, 1755.

ISAAC WOOD continued as overseer of road from Farmer's Ford to Cox's Mill, and from the meeting house to Durbin's old plantation, and from thence to James Gallon's [Gallion's] old place - November, 1755. William Cox appointed [sic].

RICHARD JOHNS continued as overseer of road from Durbin's old plantation to Lower Ferry, and from John Lyall's to Rock Run Warehouse - November, 1755.

JOHN HALL (OF CRANBURY) continued as overseer of road from Humphry's Run to John Hanson's, and from James Philips' to Rumley [Rumney?] Bridge, and from the main road by Widow Hall's to John Hall's Mill, and from said mill to Long Bridge - November, 1755.

ISAAC WEBSTER, JR. continued as overseer from Humphrey's Run to Bynam's Run, and from John Webster's to Bush Town - November, 1755. William Smith appointed [sic].

JOHN MATHEWS continued as overseer of road from Rumney Bridge to Level Bridge, and from thence until it intersects said road - November, 1755.

JAMES TAYLOR continued as overseer of road from Levell Bridge to main road by Col. Hall's Quarters at head of Swan Creek, and from thence to Swan Creek Warehouse, and from Amos Garrett's to the church - November, 1755.

WILLIAM HOPKINS continued as overseer of road from this chapple [sic] to the Quakers meeting house, and from Ephraim Gover's to Farmer's Ford - November, 1755.

EDWARD WARD continued as overseer of road from Samuel Wallace's bridge to Rock Run Warehouse - November, 1755.

WILLIAM BENNETT continued as overseer of road from Johnson's Ford to Samuel Webb's, and to his own mill, and from the chapple [sic] until it intersects the Forrest Road by Thomas Johnson, Jr. - November, 1755.

JARVIS BIDDISON continued as overseer of road from Old Road turn out to Major Franklin's in Back River Neck to head of Middle River, and from thence to N. E. Iron Works, and from thence until it intersects Old Road - November, 1755.

WILLIAM ANDREWS continued as overseer of road from head of Middle River where Jere. Biddison ends, round said river to where Daniel Scott lived, from head of said river to County Road at west end of Mr. Lawson's plantation, and from place where Daniel Scott lived up to the County Road by Lawson's Furnace - November, 1755.

JOHN SKINNER continued as overseer of road from N. E. Run to Little Valley at north end of Hatchman's house - November, 1755.

PHILIP JONES continued as overseer of road from Herring Run to bottom of Patapsco Neck - November, 1755.

JOHN MOORE continued as overseer of road from Baltimore Town Bridge, and from Jones Falls at Fell's Mill until it intersects each other and the road leading from Herring Run to bottom of Patapsco Neck below Abraham Eagleston's - November, 1755. John Woodward appointed [sic].

THOMAS STANSBURY, JR. continued as overseer of road from the Great Falls by Samuel Meredith's towards Baltimore Town until it intersects the Court Road from Richard Chinoith's toward Baltimore Town until it intersects the Court Road - November, 1755.

LOVELESS GORSUCH continued as overseer of road from Stephen Gill's to the Court Road, and from Jones Falls to William Pearce's along the Court Road - November, 1755.

JOHN BULL continued as overseer of road from Thomas Lyttlejohn's smith's shop to Thomas Richardson, Jr.'s, and from Abraham Jarrett's to Jacob Bull's Mill - November, 1755.

THOMAS DURBIN continued as overseer of road from Thomas Kelly's by James Pritchard's to Rock Run Warehouse - November, 1755.

BENJAMIN AMOS continued as overseer of road from the Fork of Winter's Run - November, 1755.

ABSALOM BARNEY continued as overseer of road from his own house to Phelphy's near the temporary line - November, 1755.

JOSEPH SMITH, at Mr. Onion's, appointed overseer of road from Buckley's to Joppa, and from thence to Little Falls at these [Onion's] Works until it intersects the main road from Joppa to the head of Bush River....Norris' old field, to be laid out according to directions of Mr. Walter Tolley and William Kitely - November, 1755.

JOSEPH MORGAN appointed in room of John West to oversee road from the lower part of Pennsylvania to Jos. Morgan's Mill on Broad Creek, and from thence to the great road that leads down to Rock Run - November, 1755.

NICHOLAS DORSEY appointed in room of John Evans to oversee road from his own house up to Frederick County - November, 1755.

WILLIAM JOHNSON appointed overseer of road from Herring Run to northside of Northeast Run, from T. L. Road [sic] to lower side of Northeast Creek at the Lancashire Works, and from Herring Run to where Patapsco Neck Road leading to Baltimore Town intersects the Main Road - November 27, 1756. William Baxter appointed [sic].

JOHN YOUNG appointed instead of Joseph Lewis to oversee road from Roger Boyce's to the run by Mr. Dean's, from Luke Stansbury's old mill place at the Great Falls by Charles Baker's to the Little Falls, and from Thomas Johnson's to Mr. Tolley's Quarters - November 27, 1756. Charles Baker appointed [sic].

EZEKIEL SLADE continued as overseer of road from Mr. Boyce's to Charlott Town, and from Boyce's to plantation where George Elliott did live, and from Josias Slade's to where John Parker lived by Little Falls, and from the wagon road from the Great Falls along by Widow Sheppard's until it intersects the wagon road from York to Joppa - November 27, 1756.

THOMAS MILES, JR. appointed instead of James Talbot to oversee road from Little Falls by John Parker's to Widow Talbot's, and from Widow Talbot's up the wagon road until it intersects the wagon road to Bush River - November 27, 1756.

JOSEPH SUTTON appointed instead of Samuel Stansbury, Sr. to oversee the Court Road from Heathcote Picket's to William Pearce's, from Stansbury's old mill place on the Great Falls of Gunpowder to Heathcote Picket's, and from mill place until it intersects the Court Road to Isaac Risteau's late dwelling plantation - November 27, 1756. Samuel Stansbury appointed [sic].

JOHN DEMMITT continued overseer of road from Widow Butler's to Baltimore Town Gateway, and from Baltimore Town Church until it intersects the road below William Lux's, and from Baltimore Town to the falls at Jonathan Hanson's old mill - November 27, 1756. Absalom Butler appointed [sic].

HEATHCOTE PICKETT continued overseer of road from Gunpowder Ferry to the little valley at the north end of lane at Mr. Lawson's Works by Hatchman's old house, from the Great Falls of Gunpowder until it intersects the county road by Roderick Cheynes, and from the Great Falls along the Court Road up opposite to said Pickett's house - November 27, 1756. Jonathan Starkey appointed [sic].

THOMAS MATHEWS continued overseer of road from Josephus Murray's to St. Thomas Church, and from there to Worthington's Mill, and Pipe Creek Road from the Great Falls of Patapsco where it crosses by said Mathews' to the Conowangoe Wagon Road - November 27, 1756. George Mathews appointed [sic].

BENJAMIN WHIPS continued overseer of road from Delaware Bottom to Digg's wagon road, then down the road to the Great Falls of Patapsco - November 27, 1756.

JOHN CROSS, SR. continued overseer of road lately laid out by Mordecai Price and John Merryman from the temporary line until it intersects Rolling Road that comes by John Merryman's to Wheeler's Mill - November 27, 1756.

RICHARD VAUGHAN appointed instead of George Ensor to oversee road from Christopher Cole's by Dennis Cole's to Stephen Price's and then to John Price's, and from Stephen Price's to Absalom Barney's - November 27, 1756.

SAMUEL HOPKINS continued overseer of road from Baltimore Town by Benjamin Bowen's until it intersects the Court Road, from Baltimore Town by Joseph Taylor's until it intersects Court Road, and from Hitcock's old field toward William Parrish's until it intersects the Court Road - November 27, 1756.

CHARLES GILBERT appointed instead of Daniel Durbin to oversee road from the Thicket Plantation to the main road by Col. Hall's Quarters, from old Gervis Gilbert's place to Howell's Mill, and from the Thicket Plantation to the main road where Doctor Wakeman formerly lived - November 27, 1756.

HENRY YOUNG continued overseer of road from Thomas Thompson's house to John Webster's - November 27, 1756.

WILLIAM COX appointed instead of Isaac Wood to oversee Quaker Road from where the road from Durbin's plantation to Susquehannah Lower Ferry crosses it by Thomas Horner's until it intersects the main road by John Critchet's from Farmer's Ford to Cox's Mill, and from the meeting house to Durbin's old plantation, and from thence to James Gallion's old place - November 27, 1756.

WILLIAM TRAPNELL appointed instead of Cornelius Brady to oversee road from Roger Boyce's to Isaac Risteau's Mill, and from said Boyce's by Richard Wilmot's to the falls by Samuel Meredeth's, and by Thomas Gittings' and John Chamberlain's until it intersects the road from Thomas Johnson's by Walter Tolley's Quarters, as it was laid out by said Tolley and Ruxton Gay, and from said Boyce's to the Great Falls where Stansbury's old mill was - November 27, 1756. Thomas Marsh appointed [sic].

STEPHEN PRICE appointed instead of Benjamin Powell to oversee road from said Price's to the Court Road, and to Wheeler's Mill to the Court Road - November 27, 1756. Aquila Carr appointed [sic].

JOHN BOREING continued overseer of road from Josephus Murray's to the temporary line - November 27, 1756.

JOHN HAMILTON continued overseer of road from William Hamilton, Sr.'s to Gwyn's Falls, from said Hamilton's by Ayer's Mill to Emmanuel Teal's, and from Widow Owings to the Dead Run - November 27, 1756.

ROBERT PATTERSON appointed instead of Thomas Mitchell to oversee road from Susquehannah to Humphry's Run - November 27, 1756. Luke Griffin appointed [sic].

GEORGE PRESBURY continued overseer of road from Winter's Run to bottom of Gunpowder Neck, and from Winter's Run to Joseph Buckley's, and from Joppa until it intersects the road from Winter's Run to bottom of Gunpowder Neck - November 27, 1756.

EDWARD LEWIS, JR. appointed instead of William Pontany to oversee road from the foot of Baltimore Town Bridge to Carroll's Mill, from Fell's Mill until it intersects aforesaid road, and from Baltimore Town to Ferry Point, and from Baltimore Forge to Baltimore Town - November 27, 1756. Valentine Larsh appointed [sic].

PATRICK MONTGOMERY continued overseer of road from Samuel Wallace's Bridge to the temporary line, and from said bridge to Ashmore's Mill - November 27, 1756.

WILLIAM PARRISH, JR. continued as overseer of road from Roger Boyce's to the Great Falls near William Rogers' plantation - November 27, 1756.

ALEXANDER MCCOMAS appointed instead of William Kitely to oversee road from the fork of road at Thomas Bond's to Otter Point, and from Winter's Run to Binam's Run, and from Bynam's Run by the meeting house to Otter Point - November 27, 1756.

HENRY GREEN appointed instead of Thomas Wheeler to oversee road from Beaver Payn's to Deer Creek by said Green's Quarters, and from Benjamin Colegate's to William Bennett's Mill, and from George Rigdon's to Widow Scott's, and from George Rigdon's to Lawrence Clark's - November 27, 1756. Daniel Preston appointed [sic].

JACOB DAVIS appointed instead of Henry Garrett to oversee road from Long Calm to Onion's Works, from thence to Mr. Dean's Run, and from thence to Col. Young's to the Long Calm - November 27, 1756.

JACOB BOND continued overseer of road from Thomas Bond's to Bull's Mill, and from Thomas Bond's to the fork of road by Beaver Pain's - November 27, 1756. Thomas Bond, Sr. appointed [sic].

GEORGE OGG, JR. continued overseer of road from his house to main falls of Patapsco, and from thence by Thomas Mathews to Frederick County - November 27, 1756.

JOHN SIMPKINS continued overseer of road from Widow Butler's to St. Thomas Church, and from thence to North Run, and from said church to Gwin's Falls and by Joseph Cromwell's and Cornelius Howard's, from Thomas Bond's to How's Mill, and from How's Mill to wagon road above Widow Butler's - November 27, 1756.

GEORGE RISTEAU appointed instead of Joseph Cromwell to oversee road from Samuel Owings until it intersects the main wagon road by Widow Butler's and from Thomas Bond's to Jones Falls, and from Monk's until it intersects the wagon road to Baltimore Town near Widow Buchanan's - November 27, 1756.

CHARLES CROXALL continued overseer of road from the head of Patapsco to Dr. Carroll's Mill on Gwyn's Falls, from thencce to Moale's Point, and from thence to the head of Patapsco - November 27, 1756.

MCLANE BAILEY continued overseer of road from Dead Run to Baltimore Forge dam, from Baltimore Works to Hunting Ridge, and from John Penn's until it intersects the road to Patapsco Falls, and from Ray Landing [Rag Landing?] to Emmanuel Teal's - November 27, 1756.

NICHOLAS ORRICK continued overseer of road from Widow Owings to Shipley's Mill from where the Court Road crosses said road to main falls of Patapsco, from main falls by Joshua Sewell's plantation until it intersects said road, and from the east side of Gwyn's Falls where John Simkins ends by said Orrick's until it intersects the main road by Jones' Quarters and the church road, and from Gwyn's Falls until it intersects the great road that leads from William Hamilton's - November 27, 1756. N. Orrick and Richard Wilmot appointed [sic].

JOSEPH NORRIS continued overseer of road from Beaver Pain's to Benjamin Norris' Quarters - November 27, 1756. Asahel Hitchcock appointed [sic].

DANIEL TREDWAY appointed instead of Thomas Bond, Jr. to oversee road from Jerusalem to Widow Talbot's, and from Edward Thorp's [Tharp's?] to Bull's Mill, and from Little Falls by John Bond's until it intersects the first mentioned road - November 27, 1756.

RICHARD DEAVER continued overseer of road from Deer Creek by his house to Thomas Crabtree's - November 27, 1756.

MOSES RUTH continued overseer of road from Capt. Paca's Quarters to John Webster's - November 27, 1756. Thomas Archer appointed [sic].

POLLARD KEEN continued overseer of road from Johnson's Ford on Deer Creek to Antill Deaver's, and from Cox's Mill to John Critchard's, and from Law. Clark's to the Thicket Plantation - November 27, 1756.

RICHARD JOHNS continued overseer of road from Durbin's old plantation to Lower Ferry, and from John Lyall's to Rock Run Warehouse - November 27, 1756. Arthur Ingram appointed [sic].

JOHN HALL (OF CRANBURY), continued overseer of road from Humphry's Run to John Hanson's and from James Philips to Rumley [Rumney?] Bridge, and from the main road by Widow Hall's to John Hall's Mill, and from said mill to Long Bridge - November 27, 1756.

WILLIAM SMITH appointed instead of Isaac Webster, Jr. to oversee road from Humphrey's Run to Bynam's Run, and from John Webster's to Bush Town - November 27, 1756. Thomas Tredway appointed [sic].

JOHN MATHEWS continued overseer of road from Rumney Bridge to Level Bridge, and from thence until it intersects said road - November 27, 1756.

JAMES TAYLOR continued overseer of road from from Levell Bridge to the main road by Col. Hall's Quarters at head of Swan Creek, and from thence to Swan Creek Warehouse, and from Amos Garrett's to the church - November 27, 1756.

WILLIAM HOPKINS continued overseer of road from this chapple [sic] to the Quakers meeting house, from Ephraim Gover's to Farmer's Ford - November 27, 1756.

EDWARD WARD continued overseer of road from Samuel Wallace's bridge to Rock Run Warehouse - November 27, 1756. Samuel Harris appointed [sic].

WILLIAM BENNETT continued overseer of road from Johnson's Ford to Samuel Webb's, and to his own mill, and from the chapple [sic] until it intersects the Forrest Road by Thomas Johnson, Jr. - November 27, 1756.

JARVIS BIDDISON continued overseer of road from the Old Road turn out to Major Franklin's in Back River Neck to the head of Middle River, and from thence to N. E. Iron Works, and from thence until it intersects Old Road - November 27, 1756.

WILLIAM ANDREW [ANDREWS] continued overseer of road from the head of Middle River where Jere. Biddison ends, round said river to where Daniel Scott lived, from head of said river to County Road at west end of Mr. Lawson's plantation, and from place where Daniel Scott lived up to the County Road by Lawson's Furnace - November 27, 1756.

JOHN SKINNER continued overseer of road from N. E. Run to Little Valley at north end of Hatchman's house - November 27, 1756.

PHILIP JONES continued overseer of road from Herring Run to bottom of Patapsco Neck - November 27, 1756.

JOHN WOODWARD appointed instead of John Moore to oversee road from Baltimore Town Bridge, and from Jones Falls at Fell's Mill until it intersects each other and the road leading from Herring Run to bottom of Patapsco Neck from Abraham Eagleston's - November 27, 1756. Josias Bowen appointed [sic].

THOMAS STANSBURY continued overseer of road from the Great Falls by Samuel Meredith's towards Baltimore Town until it intersects the Court Road from Richard Chinoith's toward Baltimore Town until it intersects the Court Road - November 27, 1756.

LOVELESS GORSUCH continued overseer of road from Stephen Gill's to the Court Road, and from Jones Falls to William Pearce's along the Court Road - November 27, 1756.

JOHN BULL continued overseer of road from Thomas Lyttlejohn's smith's shop to Thomas Richardson, Jr.'s, and from Abraham Jarrett's to Jacob Bull's Mill - November 27, 1756. Abrm. Bull appointed [sic].

THOMAS DURBIN continued overseer of road from Thomas Kelly's by James Pritchard's to Rock Run Warehouse - November 27, 1756. Henry Stump appointed [sic].

BENJAMIN AMOS continued overseer of road in the fork of Winter's Run - November 27, 1756.

ABSALOM BARNEY continued overseer of road from his own house to Phelphy's near the temporary line - November 27, 1756.

JOSEPH SMITH (Ironmaster) continued overseer of road from Buckley's to Joppa and from thence to Little Falls at Onion's Works, until it intersects the main road from Joppa to the head of Bush River (and) Norris' old field - December 1, 1757.

JOSEPH MORGAN continued overseer of road from lower part of Pennsylvania to Morgan's Mill on Broad Creek, and from thence to the great road that leads down to Rock Run - December 1, 1757.

NICHOLAS DORSEY continued overseer of road from his own house up to Frederick County - December 1, 1757.

SAMUEL STANSBURY, SR. appointed instead of Joseph Sutton to oversee the cut road from Heathcoat Pickett's to William Pearce's, from Stansbury's old mill place on the Great Falls of the Gunpowder to Heathcoat Pickett's, and from Stansbury's old mill place until it intersects the Court Road towards Isaac Risteau's late dwelling plantation - December 1, 1757.

CHARLES BAKER appointed instead of John Young to oversee road from Roger Boyce's to the run by Mr. Dean's, from Luke Stansbury's old mill place at the Great Falls by said Baker's to the Little Falls, and from Thomas Johnson's to Mr. Tolley's Quarters - December 1, 1757.

ABSALOM BUTLER appointed instead of John Demmit to oversee road from Widow Butler's to Baltimore Town Gateway, and from Baltimore Town Church until it intersects the road below William Lux's, and from Baltimore Town to the falls at Jonathan Hanson's old mill - December 1, 1757.

JONATHAN STARKEY appointed instead of Heathcoat Picket to oversee road from the Gunpowder Ferry to little valley at north end of lane at Mr. Lawson's Works by Hatchman's old house, from the Great Falls of the Gunpowder until it intersects the county road by Roderick Cheyne's, and from the Great Falls along the Court Road up opposite to Heathcoat Picket's - December 1, 1757.

GEORGE MATHEWS appointed instead of Thomas Mathews to oversee road from Josephus Murray's to St. Thomas Church, and from thence to Worthington's Mill, and Pipe Creek Road from the Great Falls of the Patapsco where it crosses by Thomas Mathews' to the Conowangoe Wagon Road - December 1, 1757.

BENJAMIN WHIPS continued overseer of road from Delaware Station to Diggs' wagon road, and then down the road to the Great Falls of Patapsco - December 1, 1757.

JOHN CROSS, SR. continued overseer of road lately laid out by Mordecai Price and John Merryman from the temporary line until it intersects the Rolling Road that comes by John Merryman's to Wheeler's Mill - December 1, 1757.

RICHARD VAUGHAN appointed overseer of road from Christopher Cole's by Dennis Cole's to Stephen Price's and then to John Price's, and from Stephen Price's to Absalom Barney's - December 1, 1757.

JOHN BOZLEY appointed instead of Samuel Hopkins to oversee road from Baltimore Town by Benjamin Bowen's until it intersects the Court Road from Baltimore Town by Joseph Taylor's until it intersects the Court Road, and from Hitcock's old field toward William Parrish's until it intersects the Court Road - December 1, 1757.

CHARLES GILBERT appointed overseer of road from the Thicket Plantation to the main road by Col. Hall's Quarters, from old Jervice Gilbert's place to Howell's Mill, and from the Thicket Plantation to the main road where Doctor Wakeman formerly lived - December 1, 1757.

HENRY YOUNG continued overseer of road from Thomas Thompson's house to John Webster's - December 1, 1757.

WILLIAM COS appointed overseer of road from Cox's Mill until it intersects the road from Rock Run by John Lyon's old house, and from said mill to Farmer's Ford on Deer Creek - December 1, 1757.

CHARLES GILBERT appointed overseer of Church Road from Cowen's old place to Obediah Pritchard's old place, and of Quaker Road from Horner's place until it intersects the road from Cox's Mill to Bush Town - December 1, 1757.

THOMAS MASH appointed instead of William Trapnell to oversee road from Roger Boyce's to Isaac Risteau's Mill, and from said Boyce's by Richard Wilmot's to the falls by Samuel Meredeth's, and by Thomas Gittings' and John Chamberlain's until it intersects the road from Thomas Johnson by Walter Tolley's Quarters as it was laid out by said Tolley and Ruxton Gay, and from said Boyce's to the Great Falls where Stansbury's old mill was - December 1, 1757.

AQUILA CARR appointed instead of Steven Price to oversee road from Stephen Price's to the Court Road, and to Wheeler's Mill to the Court Road - December 1, 1757.

JOHN BOREING continued overseer of road from Josephus Murray's to the temporary line - December 1, 1757.

JOHN HAMILTON continued overseer of road from William Hamilton, Sr.'s to Gwyn's Falls, from said Hamilton's by Ayer's Mill to Emanuel Teal's, and from Widow Owings' to the Dead Run - December 1, 1757.

LUKE GRIFFITH appointed instead of Robert Patterson to oversee road from Susquehannah to Humphry's Run - December 1, 1757.

GEORGE PRESBURY continued overseer of road from Winter's Run to the bottom of Gunpowder Neck, and from Winter's Run to Joseph Buckley's, and from Joppa until it intersects the road from Winter's Run to the bottom of Gunpowder Neck - December 1, 1757.

VALENTINE LARSH appointed instead of Edward Lewis, Jr. to oversee road from the foot of Baltimore Town Bridge to Carroll's Mill, from Fell's Mill until it intersects aforesaid road, and from Baltimore Town to Ferry Point, and from Baltimore Forge to Baltimore Town - December 1, 1757.

WILLIAM PARISH, JR. continued overseer of road from Roger Boyce's to the Great Falls near William Rogers' plantation - December 1, 1757.

ALEXANDER MACCOMAS (Carpenter) appointed instead of William Kitely to oversee road from the fork of road at Thomas Bond's to Otter Point, and from Winter's Run to Binam's Run, and from Bynam's Run by the meeting house to Otter Point - December 1, 1757.

JOHN FORWARD appointed instead of Daniel Preston to oversee road from Beaver Payn's to Deer Creek by Henry Green's Quarters, and from Benjamin Colegate's to William Bennett's Mill, and from George Rigdon's to Widow Scott's, and from George Rigdon's to Lawrence Clark's - December 1, 1757.

WILLIAM PICKETT appointed instead of Jacob Davis to oversee road from the Long Calm to Onion's Works, from thence to Mr. Dean's Run, and from thence by Col. Young's to the Long Calm - December 1, 1757.

THOMAS BOND, SR. appointed instead of Jacob Bond to oversee road from his house to Bull's Mill, and from his house to the fork of road by Beaver Pain's - December 1, 1757.

GEORGE OGG, JR. continued overseer of road from his house to the main falls of Patapsco, and from thence by Thomas Mathews to Frederick County - December 1, 1757.

JOHN SIMKIN [SIMPKINS] continued overseer of road from Widow Butler's to St. Thomas Church, and from thence to North Run, and from said church to Gwin's Falls and by Joseph Cromwell's and Cornelius Howard's, from Thomas Bond's to How's Mill, and from How's Mill to the wagon road above Widow Butler's - December 1, 1757.

GEORGE RISTEAU continued overseer of road from Samuel Owings' until it intersects the main wagon road by Widow Butler's and from Thomas Bond's to Jones Falls, and from Monk's until it intersects the wagon road to Baltimore Town near Widow Buchanan's - December 1, 1757.

CHARLES CROXALL continued overseer of road from the head of Patapsco to Dr. Carroll's Mill on Gwyn's Falls, from thence to Moale's Point, and from thence to the head of Patapsco - December 1, 1757.

MCCLAIN BAILEY continued overseer of road from Dead Run to Baltimore Forge dam, from Baltimore Works to Hunting Ridge, and from John Penn's until it intersects the road to Patapsco Falls, and from Ray Landing to Emmanuel Teal's - December 1, 1757.

NICHOLAS ORRICK and RICHARD WILMOT appointed overseers on road as Nicholas Orrick had before, from Widow Owings' to Shipley's Mill from where the Court Road crosses said road to the main falls of Patapsco, from the main falls by Joshua Sewell's plantation until it intersects said road, and from the east side of Gwyn's Falls where John Simkins' ends by Nicholas Orrick's until it intersects the main road by Jones' Quarters, and the church road, and from Gwyn's Falls until it intersects the great road that leads from William Hamilton's - December 1, 1757.

DANIEL TREDAWAY [TREDWAY] continued overseer of roads - December 1, 1757.

ASAEL HITCHCOCK appointed overseer of road from Beaver Pain's to Benjamin Norris' Quarters - December 1, 1757.

RICHARD DEAVER continued overseer of roads - December 1, 1757.

THOMAS ARCHER appointed overseer of road from Capt. Paca's Quarters to John Webster's - December 1, 1757.

POLLARD KEEN continued overseer of roads - December 1, 1757.

ARTHUR INGRAM appointed instead of Richard Johns to oversee road from Durbin's old plantation to Lower Ferry, and from John Lyall's to Rock Run Warehouse - December 1, 1757.

JOHN HALL (OF CRANBURY) continued overseer of roads - December 1, 1757.

THOMAS TREDAWAY appointed instead of William Smith to oversee road from Humphrey's Run to Bynam's Run, and from John Webster's to Bush Town - December 1, 1757.

JOHN MATHEWS continued overseer of roads - December 1, 1757.

JAMES TAYLOR continued overseer of roads - December 1, 1757.

WILLIAM HOPKINS continued overseer of roads - December 1, 1757.

SAMUEL HARRIS appointed instead of Edward Ward to oversee road from Samuel Wallace's bridge to Rock Run Warehouse - December 1, 1757.

WILLIAM BENNETT continued overseer of roads - December 1, 1757.

JERVIS BIDDISON continued overseer of roads - December 1, 1757.

WILLIAM ANDREWS continued overseer of roads - December 1, 1757.

JOHN SKINNER continued overseer of roads - December 1, 1757.

PHILIP JONES continued overseer of roads - December 1, 1757.

JOSIAS BOWEN appointed instead of John Woodward to oversee road from Baltimore Town Bridge, and from Jones Falls at Fell's Mill until it intersects each other and the road leading from Herring Run to bottom of Patapsco Neck below Abraham Eagleston's - December 1, 1757.

THOMAS STANSBURY, JR. continued overseer of roads - December 1, 1757.

LOVELESS GORSUCH continued overseer of roads - December 1, 1757.

ABRAHAM BULL appointed instead of John Bull to oversee road from Thomas Lyttlejohn's smith's shop to Thomas Richardson, Jr., and from Abraham Jarrett's to Jacob Bull's Mill - December 1, 1757.

HENRY STUMP appointed instead of Thomas Durbin to oversee road from Thomas Kelly's by James Pritchard's to Rock Run Warehouse - December 1, 1757.

BENJAMIN AMOS continued overseer of roads - December 1, 1757.

ABSALOM BARNEY continued overseer of roads - December 1, 1757.

JOHN TAYLOR (SON OF JOHN) appointed overseer of road from Joppa to Bull's Mill - December 1, 1757.

JOHN WEST appointed instead of John Wells to oversee road from the chappell adjoining John Dunn's land until it intersects near the house of John West and so down to the Susquehanna Ford called the Bald Fryer's - December 1, 1757.

ROBERT BISHOP appointed overseer of road from Buckley's to Joppa, and from thence to Little Falls at Onion's Works until it intersects the main road from Joppa to the head of Bush River (and) Norris' old field - December 1, 1758.

JAMES RIGBIE appointed overseer of road from the lower part of Pennsylvania to Joseph Morgan's Mill on Broad Creek, and from thence to the great road that leads down to Rock Run - December 1, 1758.

NICHOLAS DORSEY continued overseer of road - December 1, 1758.

WILLIAM BAXTER continued overseer of road - December 1, 1758.

WILLIAM HARWOOD appointed overseer of the Court Road from Heathcoye Picket's to William Pearce's, from Stansbury's old mill on the Great Falls of the Gunpowder to Heathcote Picket's, and from the mill place to intersection at the Court Road to ISaac Risteau's late dwelling plantation - December 1, 1758. Also added is the court order for "Col. Young and Mr. Tolley to view the road going through Samuel Stansbury's plantation to Ridgeley's Mill, and the overseer to keep it accordingly".

CHARLES BAKER appointed overseer of road from Roger Boyce's to the run by Mr. Dean's from Luke Stansbury's old mill place at the Great Falls by said Baker's to the Little Falls, and from Thomas Johnson's to Mr. Tolley's Quarters - December 1, 1758.

ABSALOM BUTLER appointed overseer of road from Widow Butler's to Baltimore Town Gateway, and from Baltimore Town Church until it intersects the road below William Lux's, and from Baltimore Town to the falls at Jonathan Hanson's old mill - December 1, 1758. Also added is the court order "for a road from Garrison Ridge to Hanson's Mill be viewed and laid out by Mr. William Rogers and John Ridgeley if not already done".

EDWARD DAY appointed instead of Jonathan Starkey to oversee road from Gunpowder Ferry to the little valley at the north end of the land at Mr. Lawson's Works by Hatchman's old house, from the Great Falls of the Gunpowder until it intersects the county road by Roderick Cheyne's, and from the Great Falls along the Court Road up opposite to Heathcote Picket's house - December 1, 1758.

SAMUEL WORTHINGTON appointed instead of George Mathews to oversee road from Josephus Murray's to St. Thomas Church, and from thence to Worthington's Mill, and Pipe Creek Road from the Great Falls of the Patapsco where it crosses by Thomas Mathews' to the Conowangoe wagon road - December 1, 1758.

JONATHAN PLOWMAN appointed overseer of road from Falls of Patapsco near Thomas Mathews to the extent of the county towards Pipe Creek - December 1, 1758.

BENJAMIN WHIPS continued overseer of road - December 1, 1758.

JOHN CROSS, SR. continued overseer of road - December 1, 1758.

RICHARD VAUGHAN appointed overseer of road from Christopher COle's by Dennis Cole's to Stephen Price's and then to John Price's, and from Stephen Price's to Absalom Barney's - December 1, 1758.

JOHN BOZLEY appointed overseer of road from Baltimore Town by Benjamin Bowen's until it intersects the Court Road, from Baltimore Town by Joseph Taylor's until it intersects the Court Road, and from Hitchcock's old field toward William Parrish's until it intersects the Court Road - December 1, 1758. Also added is "he procured Js. Brian to be appointed in his stead at March Court."

JERVIS GILBERT (SON OF MICHAEL) appointed instead of Charles Gilbert to oversee road from the Thicket Plantation to the main road by Col. Hall's Quarters, from old Gervis Gilbert's place to Howell's Mill, and from the Thicket Plantation to the main road where Doctor Wakerman formerly lived, and on Church Road from Cowen's old place to Obediah Pritchard's old place, and of Quaker Road from Horner's place until it intersects the road from Cox's Mill to Bush Town - December 1, 1758.

HENRY YOUNG continued overseer of road - December 1, 1758.

WILLIAM COX continued overseer of road from Cox's Mill until it intersects the road from Rock Run to John Lyon's old fence and from said mill to Farmer's Ford on Deer Creek - December 1, 1758.

BENJAMIN KIDD WILSON appointed overseer of road from Roger Boyce's to Isaac Risteau's Mill, and from said Boyce's by Richard Wilmot's to the falls by Samuel Meredeth's, and by Thomas Gittings' and John Chamberlain's until it intersects the road from Thomas Johnson's by Walter Tolley's Quarters, as it was laid out by said Tolley and Ruxton Gay, and from said Boyce's to the Great Falls where Stansbury's old mill was - December 1, 1758.

JOSEPH BOZLEY, JR. appointed overseer of road from Stephen Price's to the Court Road, and to Wheeler's Mill to the Court Road - December 1, 1758.

JOHN BORING continued overseer of road - December 1, 1758.

JOHN HAMILTON continued overseer of road - December 1, 1758.

LUKE GRIFFIN continued overseer of road - December 1, 1758.

GEORGE PRESBURY appointed overseer of road from Winter's Run down Gunpowder Neck to the lane between John Day's and William Hill's plantation as it formerly went to William Hill's from Winter's Run to Joseph Buckley's, and from Joppa until it intersects the road from Winter's Run to said lane, and from Bush River Ferry place until it intersects Gunpowder Neck Road on its way to Joppa - December 1, 1758.

JAMES CAREY appointed overseer of road from the foot of Baltimore Town Bridge to Carroll's Mill, from Fell's Mill until it intersects aforesaid road, and from Baltimore Town to Ferry Point, and from Baltimore Forge to Baltimore Town - December 1, 1758.

PATRICK MONTGOMERY continued overseer of road - December 1, 1758.

WILLIAM PARRISH, JR. continued overseer of road - December 1, 1758.

JOHN MACCOMUS appointed overseer of road from the fork of road at Thomas Bond's to Otter Point, and from Winters Run to Binam's Run, and from Bynam's Run by the meetinghouse to Otter Point - December 1, 1758.

IGNATIUS WHEELER appointed overseer of road from Beaver Paine's to Deer Creek by Henry Green's Quarters, and from Benjamin Colegate's to William Bennett's Mill, and from George Rigdon's to Widow Scott's, and from George Rigdon's to Lawrance Clark's - December 1, 1758.

JAMES SILVER appointed overseer of road from the Long Calm to Onion's Works, from thence to Mr. Dean's Run, and from thence by Col. Young's to the Long Calm - December 1, 1758.

JOSHUA BOND appointed overseer of road from Thomas Bond's to Bull's Mill, and from Thomas Bond's to the fork of the road by Beaver Paine's - December 1, 1758.

GEORGE OGG, JR. continued overseer of road - December 1, 1758.

JOHN SIMKINS continued overseer of road - December 1, 1758.

GEORGE RISTEAU continued overseer of road - December 1, 1758.

CHARLES CROXALL continued overseer of road - December 1, 1758.
MCLAIN BAILEY continued overseer of road - December 1, 1758.
NICHOLAS ORRICK and RICHARD WILMOT continued overseers of road - December 1, 1758.
DANIEL TREDAWAY continued overseer of road - December 1, 1758.
THOMAS LYTLE appointed overseer of road from Beaver Paine's to Benjamin Norris' Quarters - December 1, 1758.
RICHARD DEAVER continued overseer of road - December 1, 1758.
THOMAS ARCHER continued overseer of road - December 1, 1758.
POLLARD KEEN continued overseer of road - December 1, 1758.
ARTHUR INGRAM continued overseer of road - December 1, 1758.
JOHN HALL (OF CRANBURY) continued overseer of road - December 1, 1758.
JOHN WEBSTER (SON OF ISAAC) appointed instead of Thomas Tredaway to oversee road from Humphrey's Run to Bynam's Run and from said Webster's to Bush Town - December 1, 1758.
JOHN MATHEWS continued overseer of road - December 1, 1758.
JAMES TAYLOR continued overseer of road - December 1, 1758.
WILLIAM HOPKINS continued overseer of road - December 1, 1758.
SAMUEL HARRIS appointed instead of Edward Ward to oversee road from Samuel Wallace's bridge to Rock Run Warehouse - December 1, 1758.
WILLIAM BENNETT continued overseer of road - December 1, 1758.
JERVIS BIDDISON continued overseer of road - December 1, 1758.
WILLIAM ANDREWS continued overseer of road - December 1, 1758.
JOHN SKINNER continued overseer of road - December 1, 1758.
THOMAS TODD appointed instead of Philip Jones to oversee road from Herring Run to bottom of Patapsco Neck - December 1, 1758.
HUGH SOLLERS appointed instead of Josias Bowen to oversee road from Baltimore Town Bridge, and from Jones Falls at Fell's Mill until it intersects each other and the road leading from Herring Run to bottom of Patapsco Neck below Abraham Eagleston's - December 1, 1758.
THOMAS STANSBURY, JR. continued overseer of road - December 1, 1758.
LOVELESS GORSUCH continued overseer of road - December 1, 1758.
HENRY WILSON appointed instead of Abraham Bull to oversee road from Thomas Lyttlejohn's smith's shop to Thomas Richardson, Jr., and from Abraham Jarrett's to Jacob Bull's Mill - December 1, 1758.
HENRY STUMP appointed overseer of road from Thomas Kelley's by James Pritchard's to Rock Run Warehouse - December 1, 1758.

BENJAMIN AMOS continued overseer of road - December 1, 1758.

ABSOLOM BARNEY continued overseer of road - December 1, 1758.

JOHN TAYLOR (SON OF JOHN) continued overseer of road - December 1, 1758.

JOHN WEST continued overseer of road - December 1, 1758.

HENRY ADAMS appointed overseer of road from Rock Stone on Old York Road to the Temporary Line - December 1, 1758.

DANIEL POCOCK appointed overseer of road from Mr. Boyce's to Charlott Town and from Boyce's to plantation where George Elliott did live, and from Josias Slade's to where John Parker lived by Little Falls, and from wagon road from the Great Falls along by the Widow Sheppard's until it intersects the wagon road from York to Joppa at the Rock Stone - December 1, 1758.

BENJAMIN GREEN appointed overseer of road from Jas. Billingsley's to the fording place over Deer Creek near William Clark's, being the old usual road - December 1, 1758.

HENRY CROSS appointed overseer of road from Jo. Bozley's to Great Falls of Gunpowder - December 1, 1758.

JOHN GREEN, JR. appointed overseer of road from Wheeler's Mill to Jo. Bozley's, and from Wheeler's Mill to Uriah Davis', and from said mill along wagon road towards the manor to Great Falls of Gunpowder - December 1, 1758.

HENRY JAMES appointed overseer of road from Buckley's to Joppa and from thence to Little Falls at Onion's Works until it intersects the main road from Joppa to the head of Bush River (and) Norris' old fields - November, 1759.

HUGH RAY appointed overseer of road from the lower part of Pennsylvania to Joseph Morgan's Mill on Broad Creek, and from thence to the great road that leads down to Rock Run - November, 1759.

DAVID MORGAN appointed overseer of road from Joseph Morgan's Mill to the great road to Rock Run, and of the road from Bald Frier's Ferry leading to the chappell until it intersects the main road leading from Ashmore's Mill to Rock Run landing - November, 1759.

THOMAS GASSAWAY appointed instead of Nicholas Dorsey to oversee road from said Dorsey's to Frederick County - November, 1759.

WILLIAM JOHNSON appointed overseer of road from Herring Run to the north side of Northeast Run, from T. L. Road to the lower side of Northeast Creek at the Lancashire Works, and from Herring Run to where Patapsco Neck Road leading into Baltimore Town intersects the Main Road - November, 1759.

WILLIAM QUINE appointed overseer of the Court Road from Heathcote Picket's to William Pearce's, from Stansbury's old mill place on the Great Falls of the Gunpowder to Heathcote Picket's, and from the mill place until it intersects the Court Road to Isaac Risteau's late dwelling plantation - November, 1759.

CHARLES BAKER continued overseer of road - November, 1759.

WILLIAM LUX appointed instead of Samuel Merryman who had replaced Absalom Butler as overseer of road from the Widow Butler's to Baltimore Town Gateway, and from Baltimore Town Church until it intersects the road below William Lux's, and from Baltimore Town to the falls at Jonathan Hanson's old mill - November, 1759.

WALTER TOLLEY appointed instead of Edward Day to oversee road from Gunpowder Ferry to the little valley at north end of lane at Mr. Lawson's Works by Hatchman's old house, from the Great Falls of Gunpowder until it intersects the county road by Roderick Cheyne's, and from the Great Falls along the Court Road up opposite to Heathcote Pickett's house from the pines down to the free school - November, 1759.

FRANCIS WELLS appointed overseer of road from Josephus Murray's to St. Thomas Church, and from thence to Worthington's Mill, and Pipe Creek Road from the Great Falls of Patapsco where it crosses by Thomas Mathews' to the Conowago Road - November, 1759.

JONATHAN PLOWMAN appointed overseer of road from Worthington's Mill across the great Conowago Road just below Josephus Murray's towards Pipe Creek settlement - November, 1759.

ROBERT TIVIS appointed instead of Benjamin Whips to oversee road from Delaware bottom to Diggs' wagon road, then down said road to Great Falls of Patapsco - November, 1759.

JOHN CROSS, SR. continued overseer of road - November, 1759.

RICHARD VAUGHAN continued overseer of road - November, 1759.

BENJAMIN BOWEN appointed instead of John Bozley to oversee road from Baltimore Town by said Bowen's until it intersects court road, from Baltimore Town by Joseph Taylor's until it intersects court road, and from Hitcock's old field toward William Parrish's until it intersects court road - November, 1759.

BENJAMIN CULVER appointed instead of Jervis Gilbert to oversee road from the Thicket Plantation to the main road by Col. Hall's quarters, from old Jervis Gilbert's place to Howell's Mill, and from the Thicket Plantation to the main road where Doctor Wakeman formerly lived - November, 1759.

HENRY YOUNG continued overseer of road - November, 1759.

WILLIAM COX continued overseer of road - November, 1759.

WILLIAM BOZLEY appointed instead of Benj. Kidd Wilson to oversee road from Roger Boyce's to Isaac Risteau's Mill, and from said Boyce's by Richard

Wilmot's to falls by Samuel Meredeth's, and by Thomas Gittings' and John Chamberlain's until it intersects the road from Thomas Johnson by Walter Tolley's quarters as it was laid out by said Tolley and Ruxton Gay, and from said Boyce's to the Great Falls where Stansbury's old mill was - November, 1759.

JOHN COLEGATE appointed instead of Joseph Bozley to oversee road from Stephen Price's to court road, and to Wheeler's Mill to court - November, 1759.

RICHARD RICHARDS appointed instead of John Boreing to oversee road from Josephus Murray's to the temporary line - November, 1759.

JOHN HAMILTON continued overseer of road - November, 1759.

LUKE GRIFFIN continued overseer of road - November, 1759.

HENRY WETHERAL appointed instead of George Presbury to oversee road from Winter's Run down Gunpowder Neck to lane between John Day's and William Hill's plantation as it formerly went to William Hill's from Winter's Run to Jo. Buckley's and from Joppa until it intersects the road from Winter's Run to said lane, and from Bush River Ferry place until it intersects Gunpowder Neck Road on its was to Joppa - November, 1759.

JOHN MOALE appointed instead of James Carey to oversee road from foot of Baltimore Town Bridge to Carroll's Mill, from Fell's Mill until it intersects aforesaid road, and from Baltimore Town to Ferry Point, and from Baltimore Forge to Baltimore Town - November, 1759.

WILLIAM PARRISH, JR. continued overseer of road - November, 1759.

ALEXANDER MACCOMAS, JR. appointed instead of John Maccomus to oversee road from fork of road at Thomas Bond's to Otter Point, and from Winter's Run to Binam's Run, and from Bynam's Run by the meeting house to Otter Point - November, 1759.

IGNATIUS WHEELER continued overseer of road from William Clark's to Deer Creek by Henry Green's quarters, and from Benjamin Colegate's to William Bennett's Mill, and from George Rigdon's to Widow Scott's, and from George Rigdon's to Lawrance Clark's - November, 1759.

COL. WILLIAM YOUNG appointed instead of James Silver to oversee road from Long Calm to Onion's Works, from thence to Mr. Dean's Run, from thence by said Young's to the Long Calm, and from the Fork Warehouse until it intersects the forrest road above Mr. Bordley's - November, 1759.

JOSHUA BOND appointed overseer of road from Thomas Bond's to Bull's Mill, and from Thomas Bond's to fork of road by Beaver Payne's - November, 1759.

GEORGE OGG, JR. continued overseer of road - November, 1759.

CORNELIUS HOWARD appointed instead of John Simkins to oversee road from Widow Butler's to St. Thomas Church, from thence to North Run, and from said church to Gwin's Falls, and from Dr. Lyons' quarters where John Metcalf lived to Gwin's Falls, and from Thomas Bond's by Thomas Johnson's to Gwin's Falls - November, 1759.

GEORGE RISTEAU continued overseer of road - November, 1759.

CHARLES CROXALL continued overseer of road - November, 1759.

MCLAIN BAILEY continued overseer of road - November, 1759.

NICHOLAS ORRICK and RICHARD WILMOT continued overseers of road - November, 1759.

JOHN BOND (OF BUSH) appointed instead of Daniel Tredaway to oversee road from Jerusalem to Widow Talbot's, and from Edward Thorp's to Bull's Mill, and from Little Falls by John Bond's until it intersects the first mentioned road - November, 1759.

JAMES CAIN appointed instead of Thomas Lytle to oversee road from Beaver Paine's to Benjamin Norris' quarters - November, 1759.

SAMUEL LEE appointed instead of Thomas Archer to oversee road from Capt. Paca's quarters to John Webster's - November, 1759.

CORBIN LEE appointed instead of Pollard Keen to oversee road from Johnson's Ford on Deer Creek to Antill Deaver's, and from Cox's Mill to John Critchard's, and from Law. Clark's to Thickett Plantation to Benjamin Culver's - November, 1759.

HOZIER JOHNS appointed instead of Arthur Ingram to oversee road from Durbin's old plantation to Lower Ferry, and from John Lyall's to Rock Run Warehouse - November, 1759.

JOHN HALL (OF CRANBERRY) continued overseer of road from Humphry's Run to John Hanson's, and from James Phelps' to Rumley Bridge, and from the main road by Widow Hall's to John Hall's Mill, and from said mill to Long Bridge, and from Cedar Point Ferry place until it intersects the main road near Mr. Phillips' lower gate - November, 1759.

JOHN WEBSTER (SON OF ISAAC) continued overseer of road - November, 1759.

JOHN MATHEWS continued overseer of road - November, 1759.

JAMES TAYLOR continued overseer of road - November, 1759.

WILLIAM HOPKINS continued overseer of road - November, 1759.

JOHN GILES appointed instead of Samuel Harris to oversee road from Samuel Wallace's bridge to Rock Run Warehouse - November, 1759.

WILLIAM BENNETT continued overseer of road - November, 1759.

JERVIS BIDDISON continued overseer of road - November, 1759.

WILLIAM ANDREW continued overseer of road - November, 1759.

JOHN SKINNER continued overseer of road - November, 1759.

THOMAS TODD continued overseer of road - November, 1759.

HUGH SOLLERS continued overseer of road - November, 1759.

JOSEPH BANKSON appointed overseer of road from the run by Widow Gorsuch's plantation to Baltimore Town Bridge, and from the falls at Fell's Mill until it intersects the same road - November, 1759.

THOMAS STANSBURY, JR. continued overseer of road - November, 1759.

LOVELESS GORSUCH continued overseer of road - November, 1759.

WILLIAM AMOS appointed instead of Henry Wilson to oversee road from Thomas Lyttlejohn's smith's shop to Thomas Richardson, Jr., and from Abraham Jarrett's to Jacob Bull's Mill - November, 1759.

JAMES PRITCHARD appointed instead of Henry Stump to oversee road from Thomas Kelly's by said Pritchard's to Rock Run Warehouse - November, 1759.

BENJAMIN AMOS continued overseer of road - November, 1759.

ABSALOM BARNEY continued overseer of road - November, 1759.

DANIEL MACCOMUS (SON OF WILLIAM) appointed instead of John Taylor to oversee road from Joppa to Bull's Mill - November, 1759.

JOSEPH NORRIS, SR. appointed instead of Henry Adams to oversee road from Rock Stone on Old York Road to the temporary line - November, 1759.

PHILIP JACKSON appointed instead of Daniel Pocock to oversee road from Mr. Boyce's to Charlott Town, and from Boyce's to plantation where George Elliott did live, and from Josias Slade's to where John Parker lived by Little Falls, and from wagon road from Great Falls aong by the Widow Shepperd's until it intersects the wagon road from York to Joppa - November, 1759.

WILLIAM CLARK appointed instead of Benjamin Green to oversee road from Jas. Billingsley's to the fording place over Deer Creek near William Clark's, being the old usual road - November, 1759.

HENRY CROSS continued overseer of road from Jo. Bozley's to Great Falls of Gunpowder - November, 1759.

THOMAS SHEREDINE appointed instead of John Green, Jr. to oversee road from Wheeler's Mill to Jo. Bozley's, and from Wheeler's Mill to Uriah Davis', and from said mill along wagon road towards the manor to Great Falls of Gunpowder - November, 1759.

THOMAS BOND, JR. appointed overseer of road from Little Falls by John Parker's to Widow Talbott's, and from thence by the York Wagon Road until it intersects the road from York to Bush River - November, 1759.

THOMAS MEREDITH appointed overseer of road from Mr. Boyce's to Charlott Town and from Boyce's to the plantation where George Elliott did live, and from Josias Slade's to where John Parker lived by Little Falls, and from the wagon road from Great Falls along by the Widow Sheppard's until it intersects the wagon road from York to Joppa at the Rock Stone - March, 1760.

DAVID MCCULLOCK appointed instead of Henry James to oversee road from Buckley's to Joppa, and from thence to Little Falls at Onion's Works until it intersects the main road from Joppa to the head of Bush River - November, 1760.

HUGH RAY continued overseer of road - November, 1760.

RICHARD WELLS, JR. appointed instead of David Morgan to oversee road from Joseph Morgan's Mill to the great road to Rock Run, and of road from Bald Frier's Ferry leading to the chappell until it intersects the main road leading from Ashmore's Mill to Rock Run landing - November, 1760.

ABEL BROWN, SR. appointed instead of Thomas Gassaway to oversee road from Nicholas Dorsey's to Frederick County - November, 1760.

CHRISTOPHER SUTTON appointed instead of William Johnson to oversee road from Herring Run to northside of Northeast Run, from T. L. Road to the lower side of Northeast Creek at the Lancashire Works, and from Herring Run to where Patapsco Neck Road leading to Baltimore Town intersects the Main Road - November, 1760.

ISAAC RISTEAU appointed instead of William Quine to oversee the Court Road from Heathcote Picket's to William Pearce's, from Stansbury's old mill on the Great Falls of Gunpowder to Heathcote Picket's, and from the mill place to intersect Court Road to said Risteau's late dwelling plantation - November, 1760.

CHARLES BAKER continued overseer of road - November, 1760.

MAYBERRY HELMS, SR. appointed instead of William Lux to oversee road from Widow Butler's to Baltimore Town Gateway and from Baltimore Town Church until it intersects road below William Lux's, and from Baltimore Town to the falls at Jonathan Hanson's old mill - November, 1760.

WALTER TOLLEY continued overseer of road - November, 1760.

ADAM GOOSE appointed instead of Francis Wells to oversee road from Josephus Murray's to St. Thomas Church, and from there to Worthington's Mill and Pipe Creek Road from the Great Falls of Patapsco where it crosses by Thomas Mathew's to the Conowangoe Wagon Road - November, 1760.

JONATHAN PLOWMAN continued overseer of road - November, 1760.

ROBERT TIVIS continued overseer of road - November, 1760.

JOHN CROSS, SR. continued overseer of road - November, 1760.

RICHARD VAUGHAN continued overseer of road - November, 1760.

BENJAMIN BOWEN continued overseer of road - November, 1760.

WILLIAM HORTON appointed instead of Benjamin Culver to oversee road from the Thicket Plantation to the main road by Col. Hall's quarters, from old Gervis Gilbert's place to Howell's Mill, and from the Thicket Plantation to the main road where Doctor Wakeman formerly lived - November, 1760.

HENRY YOUNG continued overseer of road - November, 1760.

WILLIAM COX continued overseer of road - November, 1760.

WILLIAM BOZLEY continued overseer of road - November, 1760.

BENJAMIN POWELL appointed instead of John Colegate to oversee road from Stephen Price's to the Court Road, and to Wheeler's Mill to the Court Road - November, 1760.

RICHARD RICHARDS continued overseer of road - November, 1760.

JOHN HAMILTON continued overseer of road - November, 1760.

LUKE GRIFFITH continued overseer of road - November, 1760.

THOMAS WALTHAM appointed instead of Henry Wetheral to oversee road from Winter's Run down Gunpowder Neck to the lane between John Day's and William Hill's plantation as it formerly went to William Hill's from Winter's Run to Jo. Buckley's, and from Joppa until it intersects the road from Winter's Run to said lane, and from Bush River Ferry place until it intersects Gunpowder Neck Road on its way to Joppa - November, 1760.

JOHN MOALE continued overseer of road - November, 1760.

WILLIAM ASHMORE continued overseer of road - November, 1760.

WILLIAM PARRISH, JR. continued overseer of road - November, 1760.

THOMAS BOND, SR. appointed instead of Alex. Maccomus, Jr. to oversee road from the fork of road at said Bond's to Otter Point, and from Winter's Run to Binam's Run, and from Bynam's Run by the meeting house to Otter Point - November, 1760.

IGNATIUS WHEELER continued overseer of road - November, 1760.

COL. WILLIAM YOUNG continued overseer of road - November, 1760.

JOSHUA BOND continued overseer of road - November, 1760.

GEORGE OGG, JR. continued overseer of road - November, 1760.

CORNELIUS HOWARD continued overseer of road - November, 1760.

GEORGE RISTEAU continued overseer of road - November, 1760.

CHARLES CROXALL continued overseer of road - November, 1760.

MCLAIN BAILEY continued overseer of road - November, 1760.

NICHOLAS ORRICK appointed overseer of road from Gwin's Falls to the fork of road at Evin Jones' and from thence down the wagon road to Widow Owings', and from the falls by Igoe's to Church Road until it intersects Church Road, and then until it intersects the great road that leads from Mr.

Hambleton's from the great road by Hammond's quarters to Turnbull's Mill - November, 1760.

JOHN GOSNELL appointed overseer of road from Pontany's Mill to Evin Jones', and from thence to Shipley's Mill, and then from the great road by Peter Gosnell's through John Clark's and so to St. Thomas Church - November, 1760.

JOHN BOND (OF BUSH) continued overseer of road - November, 1760.

JAMES CAIN continued overseer of road - November, 1760.

SAMUEL LEE continued overseer of road - November, 1760.

CORBIN LEE continued overseer of road - November, 1760.

PHILIP GOVER appointed instead of Hosie Johns to oversee road from Durbin's old plantation to Lower Ferry, and from John Lyall's to the Rock Run Warehouse - November, 1760.

JOHN HALL (OF CRANBURY) continued overseer of road - November, 1760.

JAMES WEBSTER appointed instead of John Webster (of Isaac) to oversee road from Humphrey's Run to Bynam's Run, and from John Webster's to Bush Town - November, 1760.

JOHN MATHEWS continued overseer of road - November, 1760.

JAMES TAYLOR continued overseer of road - November, 1760.

WILLIAM HOPKINS continued overseer of road - November, 1760.

JOHN GILES continued overseer of road - November, 1760.

JAMES LEE, SR. appointed instead of William Bennett to oversee road from Johnson's Ford to Samuel Webb's, and to Bennett's Mill, and from the chapple until it intersects the Forrest Road by Thomas Johnson, Jr. - November, 1760.

JERVIS BIDDISON continued overseer of road - November, 1760.

WILLIAM ANDREW continued overseer of road - November, 1760.

JOHN SKINNER continued overseer of road - November, 1760.

THOMAS TODD continued overseer of road - November, 1760.

HIGH SOLLERS continued overseer of road - November, 1760.

EDWARD FELL appointed instead of Joseph Bankson to oversee road from the run by Widow Gorsuch's plantation to Baltimore Town Bridge and from the falls at Fell's Mill until it intersects the same road - November, 1760.

THOMAS STANSBURY, JR. continued overseer of road - November, 1760.

LOVELESS GORSUCH continued overseer of road - November, 1760.

WILLIAM AMOS continued overseer of road - November, 1760.

JAMES PRITCHARD contined overseer of road - November, 1760.

WILLIAM SMITH appointed instead of Benjamin Amos to oversee the road in the fork of Winter's Run - November, 1760.

ABSALOM BARNEY continued overseer of road - November, 1760.

THOMAS RICHARDSON appointed instead of Daniel Maccomus (of William) to oversee road from Joppa to Bull's Mill - November, 1760.

JOSEPH NORRIS continued overseer of road - November, 1760.

MICHAEL DURKINS [DUSKINS?] appointed instead of Philip Jackson to oversee road from Mr. Boyce's to Charlott Town and from Boyce's to plantation where George Elliott did live, and from Josias Slade's to where John Parker lived by Little Falls, and from the wagon road from the Great Falls along by the Widow Shepperd's until it intersects the wagon road from York to Joppa at the Rock Stone - November, 1760.

WILLIAM CLARK continued overseer of road - November, 1760.

HENRY CROSS continued overseer of road - November, 1760.

THOMAS SHEREDINE continued overseer of road - November, 1760.

THOMAS BOND, JR. continued overseer of road - November, 1760.

ZACCHEUS BARRET ONION appointed instead of David McCullock to oversee road from Buckley's to Joppa Warehouse to Little Falls at the Works (and) to Norris' old field until it intersects the road from Joppa to the head of Bush River - December, 1761.

HUGH RAY continued overseer of the road from the temporary line to Joseph Morgan's Mill - December, 1761.

RICHARD WELLS, JR. continued overseer of road - December, 1761.

EDWARD DORSEY appointed instead of Abel Brown to oversee the road from Nicholas Dorsey's to Frederick County - December, 1761.

JOHN ADDISON SMITH appointed instead of Christopher Sutton to oversee road from Herring Run to the north side of Northeast Run, from T. L. Road to the lower side of Northeast Creek at the Lancashire Works, and from Perring Run to where Patapsco Neck Road leading to Baltimore Town intersects the Main Road - December, 1761.

ISAAC RISTEAU continued overseer of the Court Road from Heathcot Picket's to William Pierce's from Stansbury's old mill place on the Great Falls of the Gunpowder until it intersects aforesaid road by the Piney Swamp, and to Herring Run where Valentine Larsh is building a mill, and from said old mill place to Joseph Sutton's until it intersects Court Road leading to the Long Calm - December, 1761.

ASAEL GITTINGS appointed instead of Charles Baker to oversee road from Roger Boyce's to the run by Mr. Dean's from Luke Stansbury's old mill place at the Great Falls by Charles Baker's to the Little Falls, and from Thomas Johnson's to Mr. Tolley's quarters - December, 1761.

ABSALOM BUTLER appointed instead of Mayberry Helms to oversee road from Widow Butler's to Baltimore Town Gateway and from Baltimore Town Church until it intersects the road below William Lux's, and from Baltimore Town to the falls at Jonathan Hanson's old mill - December, 1761.

WALTER TOLLEY continued overseer of road - December, 1761.

JOHN REISTER appointed instead of Adam Goose to oversee road from Josephus Murray's to St. Thomas Church, and from there to Worthington's Mill and Pipe Creek Road from the Great Falls of the Patapsco where it crosses by Thomas Mathew's to the Conowangoe Wagon Road - December, 1761.

JEREMIAH JOHNSON appointed instead of Jonathan Plowman to oversee road from Worthington's Mill across the great Conowago Road just below Josephus Murray's towards the Pipe Creek settlement - December, 1761.

ROBERT TIVIS continued overseer of road - December, 1761.

JOHN CROSS, SR. continued overseer of road lately laid out by Mordecai Price and John Harryman from the temporaray line until it intersects Rolling Road that comes by John Merryman's to Wheeler's Mill - December, 1761.

HENRY CROSS, JR. appointed instead of Richard Vaughan to oversee road from Christopher Cole's by Dennis Cole's to Stephen Price's and then to John Price's, and from Stephen Price's to Absalom Barney's - December, 1761.

BENJAMIN BOWEN continued overseer of road - December, 1761.

MICHAEL GILBERT, JR. appointed instead of William Horton to oversee road from Thicket Plantation to the main road by Col. Hall's quarters, from old Gervis Gilbert's place to Howell's Mill, and from the Thicket Plantation to the main road where Doctor Wakeman formerly lived, and on Church Road from Cowen's old place to Obediah Pritchard's old place, and of Quaker Road from Horner's place until it intersects the road from Cox's Mill to Bush Town - December, 1761.

HENRY YOUNG continued overseer of road - December, 1761.

WILLIAM WILSON appointed instead of William Cox to oversee road from Cox's Mill until it intersects the road from Rock Run by John Lyall's old place, and from said mill to Farmer's Ford on Deer Creek - December, 1761.

WILLIAM BOZLEY continued overseer of road - December, 1761.

NEAL HAIL appointed instead of Benjamin Powell to oversee road from Stephen Price's to the Court Road, and to Wheeler's Mill to the Court Road - December, 1761.

RICHARD RICHARDS continued overseer of road - December, 1761.

JOHN HAMILTON continued overseer of road - December, 1761.

WILLIAM DEBRULAR appointed instead of Thomas Walthom to oversee road from Winter's Run down Gunpowder Neck to the lane between John Day's and William Hill's plantation as it formerly went to William Hill's from Winter's Run to Jo. Buckley's, and from Joppa until it intersects the road from Winter's Run to said lane, and from Bush River Ferry place until it intersects Gunpowder Neck Road on its way to Joppa - December, 1761.

ANDREW BUCHANAN appointed instead of John Moale to oversee road from the foot of Baltimore Town Bridge to Carroll's Mill, from Fell's Mill until it intersects aforesaid road, and from Baltimore Town to Ferry Point, and from Baltimore Forge to Baltimore Town, and from the new bridge on Gwin's Falls to Baltimore Town and all streets and lanes in Baltimore Town on the west side of Jones Falls - December, 1761.

WILLIAM ASHMORE continued overseer of road - December, 1761.

JACOB GILES appointed instead of Luke Griffith to oversee road from Susquehannah to Humphry's Run - December, 1761.

WILLIAM PARRISH continued overseer of road - December, 1761.

WILLIAM KITELY appointed instead of Thomas Bond, Sr. to oversee road from the fork of the road at Thomas Bond's to Otter Point, and from Winters Run to Binam's Run, and from Bynam's Run by the meetinghouse to Otter Point - December, 1761.

THOMAS WHEELER appointed instead of Ignatius Wheeler to oversee road from Beaver Paine's to Deer Creek by Henry Green's quarters, and from Benjamin Colegate's to William Bennett's Mill, and from George Rigdon's to Widow Scott's and from George Rigdon's to Lawrance Clark's - December, 1761.

COL. WILLIAM YOUNG continued overseer of road - December, 1761.

JOSHUA BOND continued overseer of road - December, 1761.

GEORGE OGG, JR. continued overseer of road - December, 1761.

CORNELIUS HOWARD continued overseer of road - December, 1761.

GEORGE RISTEAU continued overseer of road - December, 1761.

CHARLES CROXALL appointed overseer of road from the new bridge over Gwin's Falls to the main falls of the Patapsco at the ford next above Elk Ridge Landing from Lawrance Hammond's Ferry until it intersects aforesaid road - December, 1761.

COL. BENJAMIN YOUNG continued overseer of road from the Long Calm to Onion's Works, from thence to Mr. Dean's Run, from thence by Col. Young's to the Long Calm - December, 1761.

JACOB COLLYDAY appointed instead of Nicholas Orrick to oversee road from Gwin's Falls to the fork of road by Evin Jones', and from thence down wagon road to Widow Owings', and from the falls by Igo's to Church Road, and until it intersects the Great Road leading from Mr. Hambleton's and from the Great Road by Hammond's quarters to Turnbull's Mill - December, 1761.

JOHN COOK, SR. appointed instead of John Gosnell to oversee road from Pontany's Mill to Evin Jones', and from thence to Shipley's Mill, and then from the Great Road by Peter Gosnell's through John Clark's and so to St. Thomas Church - December, 1761.

JOHN BOND (OF BUSH) continued overseer of road - December, 1761.

JOHN HUGHS appointed instead of James Cain to oversee road from Beaver Paine's to Benjamin Norris' quarters - December, 1761.

SAMUEL LEE continued overseer of road - December, 1761.

CORBIN LEE appointed (and continued) overseer of road from Johnson's Ford on Deer Creek to Antill Deaver's, and from Cox's Mill to John Chritard's, and from Lawrence Clark's to the Thickett Plantation - December, 1761.

REUBIN PERKINS appointed instead of Philip Gover to oversee road from Durbin's old plantation to Lower Ferry, and from John Lyall's to the Rock Run Warehouse - December, 1761.

JOHN HALL (OF CRANBERRY) appointed (and continued) overseer of road from Humphrey's Run to John Hanson's and from James Phillips' to Runey Ridge, and from the main road by Luke Griffin's to John Hall's Mill and from said mill to Long Bridge, and from Cedar Point Ferry place until it intersects the main road near Mr. Phillips' Lower Gate - December, 1761.

JAMES WEBSTER continued overseer of road - December, 1761.

JOHN MATTHEWS continued overseer of road - December, 1761.

JAMES TAYLOR continued overseer of road - December, 1761.

WILLIAM HOPKINS continued overseer of road - December, 1761.

JAMES LEE, SR. continued overseer of road - December, 1761.

JERVIS BIDDISON continued overseer of road - December, 1761.

WILLIAM ANDREW continued overseer of road - December, 1761.

JOHN BUCK appointed instead of John Skinner to oversee road from Northeast Run to the little valley at the north end of Hatchman's house - December, 1761.

THOMAS TODD continued overseer of road - December, 1761.

EDWARD FELL continued overseer of road - December, 1761.

THOMAS STANSBURY, JR. continued overseer of road - December, 1761.

LOVELESS GORSUCH continued overseer of road - December, 1761.

WILLIAM AMOSS continued overseer of road - December, 1761.

GEORGE BOTTS appointed instead of James Pritchard to oversee road from Thomas Kelly's by James Pritchard's to Rock Run Warehouse - December, 1761.

WILLIAM SMITH continued overseer of road - December, 1761.

ABSALOM BARNEY continued overseer of road - December, 1761.

MORRIS BAKER appointed instead of Thomas Richardson to oversee road from Joppa to Bull's Mill - December, 1761.

JOSEPH NORRIS, SR. continued overseer of road - December, 1761.

ABRAHAM RUTLAGE appointed instead of Michael Duskin [Durkin] to oversee road from Mr. Boyce's to Charlott Town and from Boyce's to plantation where George Elliott did live, and from Josias Slade's to where John Parker lived by the Little Falls, and from wagon road from the Great Falls along by the Widow Shepperd's until it intersects the wagon road from York to Joppa - December, 1761.

WILLIAM GRAFTON appointed instead of William Clark to oversee road from Jas. Billingsley's to the fording place over Deer Creek near William Clark's, being the old usual road - December, 1761.

HENRY CROSS continued overseer of road - December, 1761.

THOMAS SHEREDINE continued overseer of road - December, 1761.

THOMAS MILLS appointed instead of Thomas Bond, Jr. to oversee road from the Little Falls by John Parker's to Widow Talbott's and from thence by the York Wagon Road until it intersects the road from York to Bush River - December, 1761.

BENJAMIN RUMSEY appointed overseer of the main road from Joppa to the Little Falls of the Gunpowder - 1772.

CAPT. JOHN HOWARD appointed overseer of road from the Little Falls of the Gunpowder to Mr. Dean's Run and from said Little Falls to the Long Calm - 1772.

DANIEL BOND appointed overseer of the main road from Montgomery's Ford on Deer Creek near Capt. William Smith's to the crossroads at George McCandless' and to Chance's Mill, and from George McCandless' to York Road until it intersects the road from George Stewart's to York Town, and from McCandless' to the Little Falls by Thomas Bond's, and from Ashmead's to George McCandless' - 1772.

THOMAS BOND appointed overseer of the main road from Otter Point Warehouse to William Bay's, and from Thomas Bond's to Jacob Bull's Mill, and from Binum's Run to Otter Point Warehouse, and from the road by John Norris' to the road that goes up from the meeting house, and from Binum's Run "the new laid out road to Onion's Works which you are to open and clear" - 1772.

JAMES BRYAN appointed overseer of road from David Armstrong down to Baltimore Town Upper Bridge, and from Baltimore Town to Jonathan Hanson,

Sr.'s Upper Mill, and from thence until it intersects the main road below Job Garrison's - 1772.

THOMAS JOHNSON (OF NOD FOREST) appointed overseer of the main road from George Stewart's Tavern leading to Yorktown by the Blue Rock, and from George Stewart's to the ford of Deer Creek called Johnson's Ford, and from Webb's Ford to Timothy Neave, and from Robert Bryerly's to Job Key's, and from Corbin Lee's Forge (Deer Creek) down to John Lee Webster's lane - 1772.

CHARLES GORSUCH (SON OF CHARLES) appointed overseer of road from Charles Gorsuch's to Mordecai Price (son of Mordecai) and from thence to John Clossey's until he comes as high as Absalom Barney's plantation - 1772.

JESSE HOLLINGSWORTH appointed overseer of all public streets east of Jones Falls in Baltimore, and the road from Lower Bridge leading to Joppa by John Deaver's brick kiln to the Herring Run, and also from Upper Bridge leading to Benjamin Rogers' meadow until it intersects the above road, and also from Fell's Point to Philpott's Bridge over to Baltimore Town West Hundred, and all streets in said hundred, and all streets in Westminster, and from Baltimore Town to Ferry Point, and from said town to Carroll's Bridge and Welch's Forge - 1772.

JOHN GILL, SR. appointed overseer of road from Worthington's Mill until it intersects the main road near Josephus Murray's, and from said mill until it intersects the main road near Francis Wells' and from Stephen Gill's to the bottom of the large hill near Ledger's - 1772.

NICHOLAS DORSEY, JR. appointed overseer of road from Christopher Sewell's to Frederick County, and road from Sewell's to Punteny's Mill and Delaware Bottom Road - 1772.

BENJAMIN MERRYMAN appointed overseer of all public roads from Great Falls on the Gunpowder to York County - 1772.

JOHN HALL (SON OF JOSHUA) appointed overseer of all public roads from Wheeler's Mill on the main road leading to John Merryman, Sr.'s, and from thence to Great Falls on the Gunpowder that leads to York County - 1772.

SAMUEL DAY appointed overseer of road from George McCandless to Joppa, and from Joppa Road to Winter's Run at Jacob Bull's Mill, and from said mill to the Little Falls by John Bond's, and from Joppa Road to the Little Falls at Rock Ford, from Joppa Road to Winter's Run by Benjamin Amos', and from thence to York Road that leads from Bush Town - 1772.

THOMAS LANE appointed overseer of road from the Falls near Matthews' Mill until it intersects the public road near Daniel Bowser's, and from John Reister's to Dunkin's Mill - 1772.

JACOB MYERS appointed overseer of road above William Lux's leading to Maybury Helms' and to Stephen Wooden's, and from thence until it intersects the main road by John Price's - 1772.

PETER MILES appointed overseer of road from William Cromwell's Ford on Gunpowder Great Falls, the road leading to Larsh's Mill until it intersects the main road in Baltimore Town that comes from Towson's, from the new road on said Falls until it intersects said road, and from the ford on said Falls at Richardson's until it intersects the road which leads to Larsh's Bridge, and Old Court Road from Towson's to Long Calm - 1772.

WILLIAM GALLOWAY appointed overseer of road from "P" Hill to Nottingham Furnace, from William Andrew's Gate to the head of Middle River to main road near Nottingham Furnace on the road that leads from Nathan Nicholls until it intersects the road leading from P. Hill to Nottingham Furnace, and from Nathan Nicholls to a place called Frognorton, and the public road from "T" to John Mercer's - 1772.

THOMAS COLE, JR. appointed overseer of road from Weston Run near Dennis Garrett Cole's to Stephen Price's, from thence until it intersects the public road from Wheeler's Mill to Baltimore Town, from Weston Run near George Ensor's to Stephen Price, and from Thomas Kitten's saw mill to Quaker Meeting House, and from Thomas Kitten's saw mill until it intersects Benjamin Rogers' Road by Benjamin Wheeler's plantation formerly called Hamilton's - 1772.

GEORGE LITTLE appointed overseer of road from Widow Goodwin's up York Road to the Province Line, and from Widow Goodwin's the road that leads by Joseph Norris' to Scott's Mill, and from John Shepherd's to Hoops' Mill on the Great Falls of the Gunpowder - 1772.

JOHN BUCK appointed overseer of road from Mr. Lee's Ford on Gunpowder Great Falls and the main post road to Kingsbury Run - 1772.

JOSIAS SLADE appointed overseer of road from Benjamin Rogers' Mill to Slade's Tavern, and from thence towards York Town to Harris' Mill and from the road above Bacon Smith's Shop that leads to Cox's Ford on the Great Falls of the Gunpowder, and from thence until it intersects the main road from Wheeler's Mill to Charles Gorsuch's, and from Josias Slade's to Zachariah Strawbill's Mill on the Little Falls of the Gunpowder "that was laid by Thomas Talbott and Josias Slade to open and clear" - 1772.

CHRISTOPHER VAUGHAN appointed overseer of main road from Josephus Murray's to George Myers' - 1772.

ZACHARIAH MCCUBBIN appointed overseer of the public road from Welch's Forge along Hunting Ridge Road to Hood's Mill and to Hammond's

Ferry, and also from Miller's until it intersects the road from Hood's Mill and the new road from Ellicott's Mill until it intersects the main road from Hood's Mill to Baltimore Town, and also the new road to Hood's Mill - 1772.

JAMES BAKER appointed overseer of public road from Rebecca Clagget's to Long Calm at Mr. Lee's Ford, and from thence to Goldsmith's, and from Mr. Dean's Run to Roger Boyce's, and from Abraham Jarrett's Mill to aforesaid road, and from thence to Jeremiah Chance's - 1772.

BARNEY HOOKER appointed overseer of road from Winchester Town to Matthew's Mill - 1772.

CHRISTOPHER OWINGS appointed overseer of road from Winchester Town by Dr. Stevenson's plantation to Main Falls and from falls near Baseman's to Nicholas Jones' quarters, and from Peter Gosnel's to the road laid out by Nicholas Orrick, George Risteau and Thomas Gist near John Low's, and then to Church Road leading from Nicholas Orrick, and from said road the first crook in Samuel Owings, Jr.'s mill raise to his mill, and from the mill to the Main Road leading from John Risteau's to Baltimore Town near Mr. John Moale's plantation - 1772.

SAMUEL GRIFFITH appointed overseer of road from Mr. James Philips' plantation to the middle of Level Bridge over Mosketo Creek, and from Henry Vansickle's to the middle of Long Bridge over Cranbury Swamp near Edward Garretson's plantation - 1772.

JONATHAN WOODLAND, JR. appointed overseer of main road in Gunpowder Neck, and the road leading from Joppa to Bush Town until it intersects the road leading from thence to Baltimore Town - 1772. [Note: The name of William Robinson Presbury was first entered in the county minute book, but then was crossed out.]

JOSIAS BOWEN appointed overseer of road from the lower part of Patapsco Neck to the main road leading from Baltmore Town to Joppa and from fork of said road by Swan Harbour to Herring Run - 1772.

JOSEPH GIST appointed overseer of road from Baltimore Town to Garrison Church - 1772.

JOSEPH PERRIGOE appointed overseer of road from Weston Run at Wheeler's Mill to David Armstrong's, and from Benjamin Rogers' Mill to Weston Run at Wheeler's Mill - 1772. [Note: The name of Capt. Joshua Hall was first entered in the county minute book, but then was crossed out.]

ALEXANDER WELLS appointed overseer of road from Samuel Cookson's to Punteny's Mill, from Johannes Miller to Falls of Patapsco at Mr. Hamilton's, from Jones' quarters to Dr. Lyon's Mill, and from the mill to the main road from Jones quarter to Garrison Church - 1772.

JOHN DAUGHERTY appointed overseer of road from his plantation on the road leading by Thomas Carr's plantation until it intersects Britton Road that lead to Baltimore Town - 1772.

JAMES DEMMITT appointed overseer of roads from Mr. Boyce's to Mr. Dulany's Ford on Great Falls by William Cromwell's, and from Boyce's to Mr. Gittings' Mill, and from thence until it intersects the main road to Joppa, and from Little Falls at Rock Ford along the new road to the Great Falls - 1772.

JOHN COCKEY appointed overseer of road from bottom of hill near Ledger's until it intersects the main road below Richard Hopkins', from Walter Smith's until it intersects the road near Zekiel Towson's, and from John Pitts to Garrison Church - 1772.

STEPHEN GILL, JR. appointed overseer of road from John Price's to the line between him and George Risteau's plantation, across Aquilla Price's land until it intersects the line between Mrs. Philpot's plantation and John Gates his run, then on line between Jeremiah Johnson and Stephen Gill (son of John) to the plantation of John Price, Jr. - 1772.

EDWARD COCKEY appointed overseer of road from Samuel Owings' Gate on the Bridge until it intersects the main road near Isgrig Smith's shop, from Cookson's along Old Court Road until it intersects the road near Walter Smith's, and from Monk's Mill through Pimlicoe until it intersects the public road - 1772.

KENT MITCHELL appointed overseer of main road from Susquehanna Lower Ferry to Humphrey's Run and from Arthur Ingram's by Mount Pleasant to John Rogers' Tavern - 1772.

DANIEL ROBINSON appointed overseer of main road from Humphrey's Run to Bynam Run, and also the road leading from Bush Town to George Stewart's Tavern - 1772.

GEORGE PATTERSON appointed overseer of road from Humphrey's Run to George Stewart's Tavern, and from Dr. Carvil Hall's plantation to George Stewart's Tavern - 1772.

JOHN HAWKINS appointed overseer of all public roads in Deer Creek Lower Hundred - 1772.

IGNATIUS WHEELER, JR. appointed overseer of all public roads in Deer Creek Upper Hundred - 1772.

WILLIAM HAMMOND appointed overseer of the main road from St. Thomas Church to Joseph Murry's - 1772.

FREDERICK DECKER appointed overseer of the main road leading from George Mider's to the Province Line, towards Hanover Town, and from said Mider's to Province Line leading to York - 1772.

DANIEL ANDERSON appointed overseer of roads from Reuben Perkins' Ferry to Carson's Tavern, and from thence with the road stiled the Quaker's Road to George Stewart's at the Cross Roads, and from William Stevenson's Ferry to Carson's Tavern, and from Benjamin Herbert's plantation until it intersects the road to Cox's Mill - 1772.

ISAAC WOOD, SR. appointed overseer of roads from the place on Susquehannah above Perkins' Landing known by the name of the Pigg Landing, to Rock Run Warehouse, and from thence the main road to place where John Lathim lately lived, and from Rock Run Warehouse the main road leading to William Cox's Mill, and from thence to George Stewart's Tavern, and also the road leading from Dr. Andrews' plantation to a place called Death's Ford on Deer Creek - 1772.

WILLIAM HALL appointed overseer of main road leading from Level Bridge on Mosketto Creek to the main road at Dr. Carvil Hall's quarters on the road leading from Amos Garret's land to Spesutia Church, and on the road leading to Swan Creek Inspecting House, and to open and clear a road laid out from James Giles' quarters to Josias William Dallam's - 1772.

EDWARD HALL appointed overseer of roads leading from Humphrey's Run by Spesutia Church to James Philips' plantation and into Bush River Neck to the marked beech tree at John Hanson's plantation, and on the main road from Spesutia Church to the middle of Long Bridge over Cranbury Swamp by Edward Garretson's plantation, from James Philips' plantation to the middle of Rumney Bridge, and from where the road strikes out of the main road by James Giles' plantation to the Gander Bridge over the Cranbury Swamp, and the road leading from Humphrey's Run by John Hall of Cranberry's Mill - 1772.

THOMAS GORSUCH appointed overseer of road from David Armstrong's to Walter Dulany's Ford on Great Falls of Gunpowder, and from a place called the Over Shot Ford on Gunpowder Falls to the road leading from David Armstrong's to Walter Dulany's Ford on Great Falls of Gunpowder - 1772.

EDWARD NORRIS (SON OF JOSEPH) appointed overseer of road from Blue Rock on the wagon road by Mickenson's Mill to the Province Line - 1772.

WILLIAM PARRISH appointed overseer of road from Mr. Roger's Mill to Slade's Tavern, and from thence to Mr. Boyce's and from thence to Mr. Rogers' Mill - 1772.

[NOTE: No minutes for the years 1773 and 1774. Also, it was during this time that Harford separated from Baltimore.]

CAPT. JOHN HOWARD appointed overseer of road from Little Falls of Gunpowder to Mr. Dean's Inn and from Little Falls to Long Calm and from Mr. Dean's Inn to Long Calm - 1775.

JAMES BRYAN appointed overseer of roads from David Armstrong's to Baltimore Town Upper Bridge, from Baltimore Town to Jonathan Hanson, Sr.'s Upper Mill until it intersects the main road below Job Garrison's, and the main road by Richard Hopkins' through Charles Rogers' plantation to Jones Falls at John Stevenson's - 1775.

CHARLES GORSUCH (SON OF CHARLES) appointed overseer of road from his place to Mordecai Price (son of Mordecai), and from thence to John Clossey's to Absalom Barney's and on to George Ensor's plantation - 1775.

JOHN BARNEY appointed overseer of public streets on east side of Jones Falls in Baltimore and the road from lower bridge leading to Joppa by John Deaver's brick kiln to Herring Run, and from upper bridge leading by Benjamin Rogers' meadow, and from Fells Point to Philpott's Bridge to Baltimore Town West Hundred, and all streets in said hundred and all streets in Westminster, and from Baltimore Town to Ferry Point and from Baltimore Town to Carroll's Bridge and Welches Forge, and also the new road from Rutter's Hill to Fells Point - 1775.

JOHN GILL, SR. continued overseer of road in 1775.

JOHN ELDER appointed overseer of road from Christopher Sewell's to Ely Dorsey's plantation, and also from Sewell's to Punteny's Mill and the Delaware Bottom Road - 1775.

JOHN EVANS appointed overseer of road from Ely Dorsey's to Frederick County - 1775.

BENJAMIN MERRYMAN appointed overseer of all public roads from Wheeler's Mill on the main road leading to John Merryman, Sr.'s and from thence to Great Falls on Gunpowder that leads to York County - 1775.

JOHN CHENOWETH (SON OF ARTHUR) appointed overseer of road from the falls near Matthews' Mill until it intersects the public road near Daniel Bowser's, and also from John Rister's to Dunkin's Mill - 1775.

ABRAHAM BRITTAIN appointed overseer of road from William Cromwell's Ford on Gunpowder Great Falls leading to Larsh's Mill until it intersects the main road in Baltimore Town that comes from Towson from the new road on said Falls until it intersects said road, and from ford on said Falls at Richardson's until it intersects the road which leads to Larshes Bridge and Old Court Road from Towson's to Long Calm - 1775.

WILLIAM GALLOWAY continued overseer of road in 1775.

ELISHA DORSEY appointed overseer of all public roads from Great Falls on Gunpowder to York County - 1775.

JACOB MYERS continued overseer of road in 1775.

JOHN COCKEY OWINGS appointed overseer of roads from Weston Run near Dennis Garrett Cole's to Stephen Price's, from thence until it intersects the public road from Wheeler's Mill to Baltimore Town, from Weston Run near George Ensor's to Stephen Price's, and from Thomas Kitten's saw mill to Quaker Meeting House, and from Kitten's saw mill until it intersects Benjamin Rogers' Road by Benjamin Wheeler's plantation formerly called Hamilton - 1775.

JOHN BUCK continued overseer of road in 1775.

DIXON STANSBURY appointed overseer of roads from Slade's Tavern, the main road to Benjamin Boyce's, and from Josias Slaid's to Zachariah Strawbell's Mill on Little Falls of Gunpowder laid out by Thomas Talbott and Josias Slaid to open and clear, and from Slaid's to Little Falls by John Parker's - 1775.

JOSEPH SUTTON appointed overseer of road from the temporary line until it intersects the Harford County line - 1775.

JOSEPH NORRIS, SR. appointed overseer of road from John Dimmitt's to Abraham Scott's Mill - 1775.

NICHOLAS RICHARDS appointed overseer of main road from Josephus Murray's to George Myers' - 1775.

ZACHARIAH MCCUBBIN continued overseer of road, as in 1772, plus the road from the new bridge over Gwinn's Falls and from thence by Robert Long's plantation to main falls of Patapsco - 1775.

JESSE BUSSEY appointed overseer of public road from Rebecca Clagget's to Long Calm at Mr. Lee's Ford, from thence to Goldsmith's, and from Mr. Dean's Run to Roger Boyce's, and from Abraham Jarrett's Mill to William Standiford's - 1775.

BARNEY HOOKER continued overseer of road in 1775.

BALE OWINGS appointed overseer of road from Winchester Town by Dr. Stevenson's plantation to the main falls and from the falls near Baseman's to Nicholas Jones' Quarters, and from Peter Gosnell's to the road laid out by Nicholas Orrick, George Risteau and Thomas Gist near John Low's, and then to Church Road leading from Nicholas Orrick's, and from said road the first crook in Samuel Owings, Jr.'s mill raise to his mill, and from the mill to the main road leading from John Risteau's to Baltimore Town near Mr. John Moale's plantation - 1775.

JOSIAS BOWEN continued overseer of road in 1775.

WILLIAM KELLY, SR. appointed overseer of road from Baltimore Town to Garrison Church - 1775.

JOSEPH PERRIGOE continued overseer of road in 1775.

THOMAS GIST, SR. appointed overseer of road from the Conewagoe Road by John Read's plantation on Gwinn's Falls by Howe's Mill to Widow Owings', and from thence to Pontenany's Mill, from Johannes Miller's to falls of Patapsco at Mr. Hamilton's, from Jones' quarters to Dr. Lyons' Mill, from said mill to the main road, and from Jones' quarters to Garrison Church - 1775.
JOHN DAUGHERTY continued overseer of road in 1775.
JOHN WILSON appointed overseer of road from Mr. Boyce's to Dulany's Ford on the Great Falls by William Cromwell's, and from Boyce's to Gittings' Mill, and from thence until it intersects the main road to Joppa, and from the Little Falls at Rock Ford along the new road to the Great Falls - 1775.
JOHN COCKEY continued overseer of road in 1775.
JOHN GILL (SON OF JOHN) appointed overseer of road from John Price's to a line between him and George Risteau's plantation, across Aquilla Price's land until it intersects a line between Mrs. Philpot's plantation and John Gates' run, and then on a line between Jeremiah Johnson's and Stephen Gill's (son of John) to the plantation of John Price, Jr. - 1775.
EDWARD COCKEY continued overseer of road in 1775.
JOSEPH CROMWELL appointed overseer of the main road from St. Thomas Church to Joseph Murry's - 1775.
GEORGE EVERHART appointed overseer of the main road leading from George Mider's to the Province Line towards Hanover, and from said Mider's to the Province Road leading to York - 1775.
THOMAS GORSUCH continued overseer of road in 1775.
JOHN STANDIFORD (SON OF SKELTON) appointed overseer of roads from Benjamin Rogers' Mill to Slade's Tavern, and from the road at Burks' old fields leading to Skelton Standiford's until it comes to Benjamin Boyce's - 1775.
DANIEL CURTIS appointed overseer of roads from Armstrong's to Monkton Mill, and from Daniel Shaw's to the main road leading to the Chappel, and from the road above Bacon Smith's shop that leads to Coxes Ford on Great Falls of Gunpowder, and from thence until it intersects the main road from Wheeler's Mill to Charles Gorsuch's - 1775.
THOMAS GITTINGS, SR. appointed overseer of roads from Little Falls where Bond's Stave Road has its beginning, from thence through land of Samuel Young and Charles Baker, Sr. nearby with a road sometime ago laid out through said lands to the main road commonly called Fork Road, from thence to cross said road near the field of Mr. George Thornton and then with the road of his and Mr. Charles Wells' land commonly used about five years ago, to Mr. James Bosley's land, and through this a valley of Mr. Bosley's land and near his fence to the house of Mr. Treadway, and from the road commonly used to Thomas

Lucas' Mill, then with this mill road to land of Capt. Charles Ridgely, then with this fence to dwelling house of Henry Hendon and from said house with an old road to the Great Falls and from the Great Falls with road until it intersects below Peter Miles' at a place commonly known by the name of the White Oak Swamp - 1775.

CAPT. JOHN HOWARD continued overseer of road in 1776-1777.

JAMES BRYAN continued overseer of road in 1776-1777.

CHARLES GORSUCH appointed overseer of road from his place to Mordecai Price's (son of Mordecai) and from John Clossey's to the upper side of Benjamin Rogers' Quarters, and from said quarters to Western Run near George Ensor's on the great road leading to Baltimore - 1776-1777.

MARK ALEXANDER appointed overseer of public streets on the east side of Jones Falls in Baltimore and the road from the lower bridge leading to Joppa by John Deaver's brick kiln to Herring Run and from the upper bridge leading by Benjamin Rogers' meadow, and from Fell's Point to Philpott's Bridge to Baltimore Town West Hundred, and all streets in said hundred and all streets in Westminster, and from Baltimore Town to Ferry Point and from Baltimore Town to Carroll's Bridge and Welch's Forge, and also the new road from Rutter's Hill to Fell's Point - 1776-1777.

JOHN GILL, SR. continued overseer of road in 1776-1777.

JOHN ELDER continued overseer of road in 1776-1777.

BENJAMIN MERRYMAN appointed overseer of all public roads from Wheeler's Mill on the main road leading to John Merryman, Sr.'s, and from thence to the Great Falls on the Gunpowder that leads to York County - 1776-1777.

MORDECAI HAMMOND appointed overseer of road from the falls near Matthews' Mill until it intersects the public road near Daniel Bowser's, and also from John Reister's to Dunkin's Mill - 1776-1777.

ABRAHAM BRITTAIN continued overseer of road in 1776-1777.

WILLIAM GALLOWAY continued overseer of road in 1776-1777.

ELISHA DORSEY continued overseer of road in 1776-1777.

JACOB MYERS continued overseer of road in 1776-1777.

JOHN COCKEY OWINGS continued overseer of road in 1776-1777.

JOHN BUCK continued overseer of road in 1776-1777.

DIXON STANSBURY continued overseer of road in 1776-1777.

JOSEPH SUTTON continued overseer of road in 1776-1777.

JAMES NORRIS (SON OF EDWARD) appointed overseer of road from John Dimmitt's to Abraham Scott's Mill - 1776-1777.

NICHOLAS RICHARDS continued overseer of road in 1776-1777.

ZACHARIAH MCCUBBIN continued overseer of road in 1776-1777.
BENNETT BUSSEY continued overseer of road in 1776-1777.
BARNEY HOOKER continued overseer of road in 1776-1777.
BALE OWINGS continued overseer of road in 1776-1777.
JOSIAS BOWEN continued overseer of road in 1776-1777.
WILLIAM KELLY, SR. continued overseer of road in 1776-1777.
JOSEPH PERRIGOE continued overseer of road in 1776-1777.
THOMAS GIST, SR. continued overseer of road in 1776-1777.
JOHN DAUGHERTY continued overseer of road in 1776-1777.
SUTTON GUDGEON appointed overseer of road from Mr. Boyce's to Mr. Dulany's Ford on Great Falls by William Cromwell's, and from Boyce's to Mr. Gittings' Mill, and from thence until it intersects the main road to Joppa, and from the Little Falls at Rock Ford along the new road to the Great Falls - 1776-1777.
WILLIAM RANDALL appointed overseer of road from the bottom of the hill near Ledger's until it intersects the main road below Richard Hopkins, from Walter Smith's until it intersects the road near Ezekiel Towson's, and from John Pitts' to the Garrison Church - 1776-1777.
JOHN GILL (SON OF JOHN) appointed overseer of road from John Price's to a line between him and George Risteau's plantation, across Aquilla Price's land until it intersects a line between Mrs. Philpot's plantation and John Gates' run, and then on a line between Jeremiah Johnson's and Stephen Gill's (son of John) to the plantation of John Price, Jr. - 1776.
THOMAS HARVEY appointed overseer of road from Samuel Owings' Gate on the bridge until it intersects the main road near Isgrig Smith's shop, from Cookson's along Old Court Road until it intersects the road near Walter Smith's, and from Monk's Mill through Pimlicoe until it intersects the public road - 1776-1777.
JOSEPH CROMWELL continued overseer of road in 1776-1777.
GEORGE EVERHART continued overseer of road in 1776-1777.
BENJAMIN BOWEN appointed overseer of road from David Armstrong's to Walter Dulany's Ford on the Great Falls of Gunpowder from a place called Over Shot Ford on Gunpowder Falls to a road leading from David Armstrong's to Walter Dulany's on the Great Falls of the Gunpowder - 1776-1777.
JOHN STANDIFORD (SON OF SKELTON) continued overseer of road in 1776-1777.
DANIEL CURTIS continued overseer of road in 1776-1777.
JAMES GITTINGS (SON OF THOMAS) appointed overseer of road from the Little Falls where Bond's Stave Road has its beginning, from thence through

land of Samuel Young and Charles Baker, Sr., nearby with a road some time ago laid out through said lands to the main road commonly called Fork Road, from thence to cross said road near a field of George Thornton and then with a road of his and Charles Wells' land commonly used some years ago to James Bosley's land and through this valley of Mr. Bosley's land and near his fence to the house of Mr. Treadway, and from thence with the road now commonly used to Thomas Lucas' Mill, then with this mill road to the land of Capt. Charles Ridgely, then with his fence to the dwelling house of Henry Hendon, and from said house with an old road to the Great Falls and from the Great Falls with the road until it intersects below Peter Miles' at a place commonly called by the name of the White Oak Swamp - 1776-1777.

THOMAS G. HOWARD appointed overseer of road from the Little Falls of Gunpowder to Mr. Dean's Inn, from Little Falls of Long Calm, and from Mr. Dean's Inn to Long Calm - 1778.

JOSHUA STEVENSON appointed overseer of road from David Armstrong's to Baltimore Town Upper Bridge, from Baltimore Town to Jonathan Hanson, Sr.'s Upper Mill until it intersects the main road below Job Garrison's, and the main road by Richard Hopkins' through Charles Rogers' plantation to Jones Falls at John Stevenson's - 1778.

CAPT. JOSHUA HALL appointed overseer of road from Charles Gorsuch's (son of Charles) to Mordecai Price's (son of Mordecai) and from thence to John Clossey's to Abalsom Barney's and on to George Ensor's plantation - 1778.

JOHN GILL, SR. continued overseer of road in 1778.

JAMES STERETT appointed overseer of public streets on the east side of Jones Falls in Baltimore and the road from the lower bridge leading to Joppa by John Deaver's brick kiln to Herring Run -1778.

ABEL BROWN, SR. appointed overseer of road from Christopher Sewell's to Ely Dorsey's plantation and also from Sewell's to Punteney's Mill and the Delaware Bottom Road - 1778.

BENJAMIN LAWRENCE appointed overseer of road from Ely Dorsey's to Frederick County - 1778.

BENJAMIN MERRYMAN continued overseer of road in 1778.

JOHN REISTER appointed overseer of road from the falls near Matthews' Mill until it intersects the public road near Daniel Bowser's, and also from John Rister's to Dunkin's Mill - 1778.

ABRAHAM BRITTAIN continued overseer of road in 1778.

WILLIAM NICHOLSON appointed overseer of road from "P" Hill to Nottingham Furnace, from William Andrew's Gate to the head of Middle River to the main road near Nottingham Furnace on the road leading from Nathan Nicholls' until it intersects the road leading from "P" Hill to Nottingham Furnace, and from Nathan Nicholls' to a place called Frognorton, and the public roads from "T" to John Mercer's - 1778.

WILLIAM HOOFMAN (Paper Miller) appointed overseer of all public roads from the Great Falls on Gunpowder to York County - 1778.

JACOB MYERS continued overseer of road in 1778.

JOHN COCKEY OWINGS continued overseer of road in 1778.

BENJAMIN BUCK appointed overseer of road from Lee's Ford on the Gunpowder Great Falls and the main Post Road to Kingsburry Run - 1778.

DIXON STANSBURY continued overseer of road in 1778.

JOSEPH SUTTON continued overseer of road in 1778.

JOHN BACON appointed overseer of road from John Dimmitt's to Abraham Scott's Mill - 1778.

AMON BUTLER, JR. appointed overseer of the main road from Josephus Murrey's to George Myers' - 1778.

ZACHARIAH MCCUBBIN continued overseer of road in 1778.

BENNETT BUSSEY appointed overseer of public roads from Rebecca Clagget's to the Long Calm at Mr. Lee's Ford, from thence to Goldsmith's, and from Mr. Dean's Run to Roger Boyce's, and from Abraham Jarrett's Mill to aforesaid road and from thence to Jeremiah Chance's - 1778.

SAMUEL CHENOWETH appointed overseer of road from Winchester Town to Matthews' Mill - 1778.

THOMAS LANE appointed overseer of road from Winchester Town by Dr. Stevenson's plantation to the Main Falls and from the falls near Baseman's to Nicholas Jones' Quarters, and from Peter Gosnell's to the road laid out by Nicholas Orrick, George Risteau and Thomas Gist near John Low's, then to Church Road leading from Nicholas Orrick's, and from said road the first crook in Samuel Owings, Jr.'s mill raise to his mill, and from the mill to the Main Road leading from John Risteau's to Baltimore Town near John Moale's plantation -1778.

JOSIAS BOWEN continued overseer of road in 1778.

WILLIAM KELLY, SR. appointed overseer of road from Baltimore Town to the Garrison Church - 1778.

EDWARD TALBOTT appointed overseer of road from Weston Run at Wheeler's Mill to David Armstrong's, and from Benjamin Rogers' Mill to Weston Run at Wheeler's Mill - 1778.

THOMAS GIST, SR. continued overseer of road in 1778.

HENRY SATER appointed overseer of road from John Daugherty's plantation on the road leading by Thomas Carr's plantation until it intersects Britton Road that leads to Baltimore Town - 1778.

SUTTON GUDGEON appointed overseer of road from Mr. Boyce's to Mr. Dulaney's Ford on the Great Falls by William Cromwell's and from Boyce's to Mr. Gittings' Mill, and from thence until it intersects the main road to Joppa, and from the Little Falls at Rock Ford along the main road to the Great Falls - 1778.

WILLIAM RANDELL continued overseer of road in 1778.

JOHN GILL (SON OF JOHN) continued overseer of road in 1778.

THOMAS HARVEY continued overseer of road in 1778.

STEPHEN CROMWELL continued overseer of road in 1778. [Note: There is no prior entry for Stephen Cromwell, but from earlier entries it appears he replaced Joseph Cromwell].

GEORGE EVERHART continued overseer of road in 1778.

SOLOMON BOWEN continued overseer of road in 1778.

JOHN STANDIFORD (OF JNO.) continued overseer of road in 1778.

EDMUND STANSBURY continued overseer of road in 1778.

[Note: All entries for overseers of roads in 1780 were crossed out in Minutes Book No. 4 on pages 405 to 412. Therefore, the following entries have two dates per name, with some exceptions, and thus assuming the same men were reappointed in 1780 after having served in 1779 as well. Perhaps the on-going Revolutionary War had something to do with who was appointed based on who was available to serve].

THOMAS G. HOWARD continued overseer of road in 1779-1780.

WILLIAM COLE appointed instead of Joshua Stevenson to oversee road from David Armstrong's to Baltimore Town Upper Bridge, from Baltimore Town to Jonathan Hanson, Sr.'s Upper Mill until it intersects the main road below Job Garrison's, and the main road by Richard Hopkins' through Charles Rogers' plantation to Jones Falls at John Stevenson's - 1779-1780.

BENJAMIN HOOKER appointed overseer of road from John Green's to Capt. Joshua Hall's Mill, from thence leaving Benjamin Hooker's until it intersects the road near Benjamin Wheeler's fence, and from thence to John Clossey's as far as the upper side of Benjamin Roger's Quarters, and from said quarters to Western Run near George Ensor's on the great road leading to Baltimore - 1779-1780.

JOHN PITTS appointed overseer of road from Worthington's Mill until it intersects the main road near Josephus Murray's, and from said mill until it intersects the main road near Francis Wells', and from Stephen Gill's to the bottom of the large hill near Ledger's - 1779-1780.

JAMES LYSTON appointed instead of James Sterrett to oversee the public streets on the east side of Jones Falls in Baltimore, and the road from the lower bridge leading to Joppa by John Deaver's brick kiln to Herring Run - 1779-1780.

ABEL BROWN, SR. continued overseer of road in 1779-1780.

BENJAMIN LAWRENCE continued overseer of road in 1779-1780.

BENJAMIN MERRYMAN continued overseer of road in 1779-1780.

JOHN GRIFFITH appointed overseer of road from the falls near Matthews' Mill until it intersects the public road near Daniel Bowser's, and also from John Rister's to Dunkins' Mill - 1779-1780.

ABRAHAM BRITTAIN continued overseer of road in 1779-1780.

NATHAN NICHOLSON appointed instead of William Nicholson to oversee road from "P" Hill to Nottingham Furnace, from William Andrew's Gate to the head of Middle River to the main road near Nottingham Furnace on the road leading from Nathan Nicholls' until it intersects the road leading from "P" Hill, and from Nathan Nicholls' to a place called Frognorton, and the public road from "T" to John Mercer's - 1779-1780.

WILLIAM HOOFMAN continued overseer of road in 1779-1780.

JACOB MYERS continued overseer of road in 1779-1780.

JOHN COCKEY OWINGS continued overseer of road in 1779-1780.

JOHN SKINNER appointed instead of Benjamin Buck to oversee road from Mr. Lee's Ford on Gunpowder Great Falls and the main post road to Kingsbury Run - 1779-1780.

DIXON STANSBURY continued overseer of road in 1779-1780.

JOSEPH SUTTON continued overseer of road in 1779-1780.

JOHN BACON continued overseer of road in 1779-1780.

AMON BUTLER, JR. continued overseer of road in 1779-1780.

ZACHARIAH MCCUBBIN continued overseer of road in 1779-1780.

JOHN BARROW, JR. appointed overseer of public road from Rebecca Clagget's to Long Calm at Mr. Lee's Ford, from thence to Goldsmith's and from Mr. Dean's Run to Roger Boyce's, and from Abraham Jarrett's Mill to aforesaid road and from thence to Jeremiah Chance's - 1779-1780.

SAMUEL CHENOWITH continued overseer of road in 1779-1780.

THOMAS LANE continued overseer of road in 1779-1780.

JOSIAS BOWEN continued overseer of road in 1779-1780.

WILLIAM KELLY, SR. continued overseer of road in 1779-1780.

EDWARD TALBOTT continued overseer of road in 1779-1780.

THOMAS GIST, SR. continued overseer of road in 1779-1780.

HENRY SATER continued overseer of road in 1779. [Note: In the minute book this entry was made and then crossed out].

SUTTON GUDGEON continued overseer of road in 1779-1780.

HENRY GUDGEON appointed instead of Sutton Gudgeon to oversee road from Mr. Boyce's to Mr. Dulany's Ford on the Great Falls by William Cromwell's, and from Boyce's to Gittings' Mill, and from thence until it intersects the main road to Joppa, and from the Little Falls at Rock Ford along the new road to the Great Falls - 1779-1780.

SAMUEL HUNT appointed overseer of road from the bottom of the hill near Ledger's until it intersects the main road below Richard Hopkins', from Walter Smith's until it intersects the road near Zekiel Towson's, and from John Pitts' to Garrison Church - 1779-1780.

JOHN GILL (SON OF JOHN) continued overseer of road in 1779-1780.

THOMAS HARVEY continued overseer of road in 1779-1780.

AMON BUTLER, SR. appointed instead of Stephen Cromwell to oversee the main road from St. Thomas Church to Joseph Murry's - 1779-1780.

GEORGE EVERHART continued overseer of road in 1779-1780.

SOLOMON BOWEN continued overseer of road in 1779-1780.

JOHN STANDIFORD (OF JNO.) continued overseer of road in 1779-1780.

EDMUND STANSBURY continued overseer of road in 1779-1780.

JAMES GITTINGS (SON OF THOMAS) continued overseer of road in 1779-1780.

THOMAS HOWARD continued overseer of road in 1781-1782.

WILLIAM COLE continued overseer of road in 1781-1782.

BENJAMIN HOOKER continued overseer of road in 1781-1782.

JOHN PITTS continued overseer of road in 1781-1782.

JAMES LYSTON continued overseer of road in 1781-1782.

ABEL BROWN, SR. continued overseer of road in 1781-1782.

BENJAMIN LAWRENCE continued overseer of road in 1781-1782.

BENJAMIN MERRYMAN continued overseer of road in 1781-1782.

JOHN GRIFFITH continued overseer of road in 1781-1782.

ABRAM BRITTAIN continued overseer of road in 1781-1782.

NATHAN NICHOLSON continued overseer of road in 1781-1782.

JAMES CAMPBELL appointed instead of William Hoofman to oversee all public roads from the Great Falls on the Gunpowder to York County - 1781-1782.

MAYBERRY HELMS appointed instead of Jacob Myers to oversee road from above William Lux's leading to said Helm's and to Stephen Wooden's, and from thence until it intersects the main road by John Price's - 1781-1782.

STEPHEN PRICE appointed instead of John Cockey Owings to oversee road from Weston Run near Dennis Garrett Cole's to Stephen Price's, from thence until it intersects the public road from Wheeler's Mill to Baltimore Town, from Weston Run near George Ensor's to Stephen Price's, and from Thomas Kitten's saw mill to the Quaker Meeting House, and from Kitten's Mill until it intersects Benjamin Rogers' road by Benjamin Wheeler's plantation formerly called Hamilton's - 1781-1782.

JOHN SKINNER continued overseer of road in 1781-1782.

DIXON STANSBURY continued overseer of road in 1781-1782.

JOSEPH SUTTON continued overseer of road in 1781-1782.

JOHN BACON continued overseer of road in 1781-1782.

AMON BUTLER, JR. continued overseer of road in 1781-1782.

EDWARD TEAL appointed instead of Zachariah McCubbin to oversee public roads from Welch's Forge along Hunting Ridge Road to Hood's Mill and to Hammond's Ferry, and also from Miller's until it intersects the road from Hood's Mill, the new road from Ellicott's Mill until it intersects the main road from Hood's Mill to Baltimore Town, and also the new road to Hood's Mill - 1781-1782.

JOHN BARROW, JR. continued overseer of road in 1781-1782.

SAMUEL CHENOWITH continued overseer of road in 1781-1782.

SAMUEL OWINGS (OF SAMUEL) appointed instead of Thomas Lane to oversee road from Winchester Town by Dr. Stevenson's plantation to the Main Falls and from the falls near Baseman's to Nicholas Jones' Quarters, and from Peter Gosnell's to the road laid out by Nicholas Orrick, George Risteau, and Thomas Gist near John Low's, then to Church Road leading from Nicholas Orrick's, and from said road the first crook in Samuel Owings, Jr.'s mill raise to his mill, and from the mill to the Main Road leading from John Risteau's to Baltimore Town near John Moale's plantation - 1781-1782.

JOSIAS BOWEN continued overseer of road in 1781-1782.

WILLIAM KELLY, SR. continued overseer of road in 1781-1782.

BENJAMIN TALBOTT (OF EDWARD) appointed instead of Edward Talbott to oversee road from Weston Run at Wheeler's Mill to David Armstrong's, and from Benjamin Rogers' Mill to Weston Run at Wheeler's Mill - 1781-1782.

SOLOMON ALLEN appointed instead of Thomas Gist, Sr. to oversee road from the Conewagoe Road by John Read's plantation over Gwinn's Falls by Howe's Mill to Widow Owings' and from thence to Pontenay's Mill, from

Johannes Miller's to the falls of the Patapsco, from the mill to the main road, and from Jones' Quarters to Garrison Church - 1781-1782.

SUTTON GUDGEON appointed instead of Henry Gudgeon to oversee road from Mr. Boyce's to Mr. Dulany's Ford on the Great Falls by William Cromwell's, and from Boyce's to Mr. Gittings' Mill, and from thence until it intersects the main road to Joppa, and from the Little Falls at Rock Ford along the new road to the Great Falls - 1781-1782.

SAMUEL HUNT continued overseer of road in 1781-1782.

JOHN GILL (SON OF JOHN) continued overseer of road in 1781-1782.

EDWARD COCKEY appointed instead of Thomas Harvey to oversee road from Samuel Owings' Gate on the bridge until it intersects the main road near Isgrig Smith's shop, from Cookson's along Old Court Road until it intersects the road near Walter Smith's, and from Monk's Mill through Pimlicoe until it intersects the public road - 1781-1782.

AMON BUTLER, SR. continued overseer of road in 1781-1782.

GEORGE EVERHART continued overseer of road in 1781-1782.

WALTER BOSLEY appointed instead of Solomon Bowen to oversee road from David Armstrong's to Walter Dulany's Ford on the Great Falls of Gunpowder, and from a place called the Over Shot Ford on Gunpowder Falls to the road leading from David Armstrong's to Walter Dulany's Ford on the Great Falls of the Gunpowder - 1781-1782.

JOHN STANDIFORD (OF JNO.) continued overseer of road in 1781-1782.

EDMUND STANSBURY continued overseer of road in 1781-1782.

JAMES GITTINGS (SON OF THOMAS) continued overseer of road in 1781-1782.

WILLIAM HOBBY appointed overseer of road from the new bridge across Gwinn's Falls to Lawrence Hammond's Ferry, and from said bridge to the main falls of Patapsco by Robert Long's plantation - 1781-1782.

JOSHUA STEVENSON appointed instead of William Cole to oversee road from David Armstrong's to Baltimore Town Upper Bridge, from Baltimore Town to Jonathan Hanson, Sr.'s Upper Mill until it intersects the main road below Job Garrison's, and the main road by Richard Hopkins' through Charles Rogers' plantation to Jones Falls at John Stevenson's - 1782.

BENJAMIN HOOKER appointed overseer of road to John Clossey's as far as Nicholas Merryman's fence - 1782. [See previous entries for Benjamin Hooker to see how road description changed, with part of it being assigned to George Ensor].

GEORGE ENSOR appointed overseer of road from Western Run at said Ensor's to the upper edge of Benjamin Rogers, Esq.'s Quarters, and on to

Jonathan Tipton's across the Barrens to Anthony Null's as laid out by said Jonathan Tipton and Robert Lemmon - 1782.

JOHN MCDONOGH appointed instead of James Lyston to oversee the public streets on the east side of Jones Falls in Baltimore, and from the Lower Bridge leading to Joppa by John Deaver's brick kiln to Herring Run - 1782.

PETER TEVIS appointed instead of Abel Brown, Sr. to oversee road from Christopher Sewell's to Ely Dorsey's plantation, and also from Sewell's to Punteney's Mill and the Delaware Bottom Road - 1782.

JOHN GRIFFITH continued overseer of road in 1782. [Note: The same description is given except Dunkin's Mill in previous descriptions is now referred to as Hudson's Mill].

NICHOLAS BRITTAIN appointed instead of Abraham Brittain to oversee road from William Cromwell's Ford on Gunpowder Great Falls to the road leading to Larsh's Mill until it intersects the main road in Baltimore Town that comes from Towson's, from the new road on said falls until it intersects said road, and from the ford on said falls at Richardson's until it intersects the road which leads to Larsh's Bridge, and Old Court Road from Towson's to the Long Calm - 1782.

WILLIAM HARVEY appointed instead of Stephen Price to oversee road from Weston Run near Dennis Garrett Cole's to Stephen Price's, from thence until it intersects the public road from Wheeler's Mill to Baltimore Town, from Weston Run near George Ensor's to Stephen Price's, and from Thomas Kitten's saw mill to Quaker Meeting House, and from Kitten's Mill until it intersects Benjamin Rogers' Road by Benjamin Wheeler's plantation formerly called Hamilton's - 1782.

HENRY HOWARD appointed instead of John Skinner to oversee road from Lee's Ford on the Gunpowder Great Falls, and the main Post Road to Kingsbury Run - 1782.

JACOB HOOK, SR. appointed instead of William Kelly, Sr. to oversee road from Slade's Tavern on the main road to Benjamin Boyce's, and from Josias Slaid's to Zachariah Strawbell's Mill on the Little Falls of Gunpowder laid out by Thomas Talbott and Josias Slaid to open and clear, and from Slaid's to the Little Falls by John Parker's - 1782.

AMOS OGDEN appointed instead of Benjamin Talbott to oversee road from Weston Run at Wheeler's Mill to David Armstrong's, and from Benjamin Rogers' Mill to Weston Run at Wheeler's Mill - 1782.

THOMAS HOWARD continued overseer of road in 1783.

NICHOLAS HOPKINS appointed instead of Joshua Stevenson to oversee road in 1783.

MORDECAI PRICE (OF MORDECAI) appointed instead of Benjamin Hooker to oversee road in 1783, and reappointed in 1784.

GEORGE ENSOR continued overseer of road in 1783-1784.

JOSEPH OSBURN appointed instead of John Pitts to oversee road in 1783, and reappointed in 1784.

JACOB MYERS appointed instead of John McDonogh and David Shields to oversee the road to Philpott's Bridge and to Calvert Street, and also the new road from Rutter's Mill to Fell's Point - 1783.

PETER TEVIS continued overseer of road in 1783-1784.

BENJAMIN LAWRENCE continued overseer of road in 1783-1784.

JOHN FOSTER appointed instead of Benjamin Merryman to oversee all public roads from Wheeler's Mill on the main road leading to John Merryman, Sr.'s, and from thence to the Great Falls on Gunpowder that leads to York County - 1783, and reappointed in 1784.

JOHN GRIFFITH continued overseer of road in 1783-1784.

NICHOLAS BRITTAIN continued overseer of road in 1783-1784.

NATHAN NICHOLSON continued overseer of road in 1783-1784.

JAMES CAMPBELL continued overseer of road in 1783-1784.

MAYBERRY HELMS continued overseer of road in 1783-1784.

WILLIAM HARVEY continued overseer of road in 1783-1784.

WILLIAM ALLENDER (OF JOSEPH) appointed instead of Henry Howard and John Buck to oversee the road from Lee's Ford on Gunpowder Great Falls, and the main Post Road to Kingsbury Run - 1783.

DIXON STANSBURY continued overseer of road in 1783-1784.

JOSEPH SUTTON continued overseer of road in 1783-1784.

JOHN BACON continued overseer of road in 1783.

AMON BUTLER, JR. continued overseer of road in 1783-1784.

EDWARD TEAL continued overseer of road in 1783.

JOHN BARROW, JR. continued overseer of road in 1783-1784.

SAMUEL CHENOWITH continued overseer of road in 1783-1784.

SAMUEL OWINGS (OF SAMUEL) continued overseer of road in 1783-1784.

THOMAS KNIGHT SMITH SHAW appointed instead of Josias Bowen to oversee road from the lower part of Patapsco Neck to the main road leading from Baltimore Town to Joppa, and from the fork of the road by Swan Harbour to Herring Run - 1783, and reappointed in 1784.

JACOB HOOK continued overseer of road in 1783-1784.

AMOS OGDEN continued overseer of road in 1783.

JOHN SWINGLE appointed instead of Solomon Allen to oversee roads from the Conewago Road by John Read's plantation over Gwinn's Falls by Howe's Mill to Widow Owings', and from thence to Pontenay's Mill, from Johannes Miller's to the falls of the Patapsco at Mr. Hamilton's, from Jones' Quarter to Dr. Lyon's Mill, from the mill to the main road, and from Jones' Quarter to Garrison Church - 1783, and reappointed in 1784.

THOMAS FRANKLIN, JR. appointed instead of Sutton Gudgeon to oversee road from Mr. Boyce's to Dulany's Ford on the Great Falls by William Cromwell's, and from Boyce's to Gittings' Mill, and from thence until it intersects the main road to Joppa, and from the Little Falls at Rock Ford along the new road to the Great Falls - 1783.

SAMUEL HUNT continued overseer of road in 1783.

JOHN GILL (SON OF JOHN) continued overseer of road in 1783-1784.

MICHAEL KRANER appointed instead of Edward Cockey to oversee road from Samuel Owings' Gate near the bridge until it intersects the main road near Isgrig Smith's Shop, from Cookson's along Old Court Road until it intersects the road near Walter Smith's, and from Monk's Mill through Pimlicoe until it intersects the public road - 1783, and reappointed in 1784.

WALTER BOSLEY continued overseer of road in 1783-1784.

JOHN STANDIFORD (OF JNO.) continued overseer of road in 1783-1784.

WILLIAM SLADE (OF JOSIAS) appointed instead of Edmund Stansbury to oversee road in 1783, and reappointed in 1784.

JAMES GITTINGS continued overseer of road in 1783-1784.

WILLIAM HOBBY continued overseer of road in 1783.

DAVID POE appointed overseer of road from the west side of Calvert Street in Baltimore Town to the ferry point, and from said town to Carroll's Bridge and Welsh's Forge - 1783.

WILLIAM DEMMITT appointed instead of Thomas Howard to oversee road in 1784.

JOHN ENSOR (OF ABRAHAM) appointed instead of Nicholas Hopkins to oversee road in 1784.

GEORGE HELMS appointed instead of Jacob Myers to oversee road in 1784.

GEORGE LEGGETT appointed instead of William Allender to oversee road in 1784.

DANIEL SHAW appointed instead of John Bacon to oversee road in 1784.

JOHN ELLICOTT appointed instead of Edward Teal to oversee road in 1784.

BENJAMIN BOWEN appointed instead of Amos Ogden to oversee road in 1784.

JOHN CHAMBERLAIN appointed instead of Thomas Franklin, Jr. to oversee road in 1784.

CAPT. JOHN COCKEY appointed instead of Samuel Hunt to oversee road in 1784.

AMON BUTLER, SR. continued overseer of road in 1784.

MICHAEL FISHER continued overseer of road in 1784.

SAMUEL NORWOOD appointed instead of William Hobby to oversee road in 1784. DAVID POE continued overseer of road in 1784.

WILLIAM DEMMITT continued overseer of road in 1785-1786.

JOHN HOPKINS appointed instead of John Ensor to oversee road in 1785.

MORDECAI PRICE continued overseer of road in 1785-1786.

JOSEPH STANSBURY appointed instead of George Ensor to oversee road in 1785.

JOSEPH OSBURN continued overseer of road in 1785-1786.

PETER LIDDICK appointed instead of George Helms to oversee road in 1785, and reappointed in 1786.

FRANCIS SNOWDEN appointed instead of Peter Tevis to oversee road in 1785.

JOHN EVANS appointed instead of Benjamin Lawrence to oversee road in 1785.

CHARLES GORSUCH (OF CHARLES) appointed instead of John Foster to oversee road in 1785, and reappointed in 1786.

JOHN GRIFFITH continued overseer of road in 1785-1786.

NICHOLAS BRITTAIN continued overseer of road in 1785-1786.

WALTER DALLIS appointed instead of Nathan Nicholson to oversee road from John Mercer Porter's to "T" from head of Middle River to intersects main road that leads to said Porter's to "T" from head of Middle River to "T" at Widow Fowler's" - 1785.

JAMES CAMPBELL continued overseer of road in 1785-1786.

GEORGE G. PRESBURY, JR. appointed overseer of road from "P" Hill to Nottingham Furnace from William Andrews' Gate to the head of Middle River to the main road near Nottingham Furnace on the road leading from Nathan Nicholls until it intersects the road leading from "P" Hill to Nottingham Furnace, and from Nathan Nicholls' to a place called Frognorton, and the public road from "T" to John Mercer's - 1785.

WILLIAM STENSON appointed instead of Mayberry Helms to oversee road in 1785.

WILLIAM HARVEY continued overseer of road in 1785-1786.

GABRIEL P. VANHORN appointed instead of George Leggett to oversee road in 1785. [Note: Road description wording changed from what formerly read "Kingsbury" to what now reads "Philpott's Ridge in Baltimore Town"].

DIXON STANSBURY continued overseer of road in 1785-1786.

JOSEPH SUTTON continued overseer of road in 1785-1786.

DANIEL SHAW continued overseer of road in 1785. [Note: Although he appears to have been reappointed in 1786, the entry is crossed out of Minute Book No. 5 on page 391].

AMON BUTLER, JR. continued overseer of road in 1785-1786.

JOHN ELLICOTT continued overseer of road in 1785-1786.

JOHN BARROW, JR. continued overseer of road in 1785.

SAMUEL CHENOWITH continued overseer of road in 1785-1786.

SAMUEL OWINGS continued overseer of road in 1785-1786.

PATRICK LYNCH appointed instead of Thomas Knight Smith Shaw to oversee road in 1785, and reappointed in 1786.

GEORGE BEAM appointed instead of Jacob Hook to oversee road in 1785.

BENJAMIN ROGERS appointed instead of Benjamin Bowen and Robert Wilmott to oversee road in 1785.

THOMAS GREENWOOD appointed instead of John Swingle to oversee road in 1785, and reappointed in 1786.

JOHN CHAMBERLAIN continued overseer of road in 1785-1786.

CAPT. JOHN COCKEY continued overseer of road in 1785-1786.

JOHN GRIFFITH continued overseer of road in 1785-1786.

THOMAS HARVEY appointed instead of Michael Kraner to oversee road in 1785.

AMON BUTLER, SR. continued overseer of road in 1785-1786.

JOHN SHOWERS appointed instead of Michael Fisher to oversee road in 1785, and reappointed in 1786.

WALTER BOSLEY continued overseer of road in 1785-1786.

JOHN STANDIFORD (OF JNO.) continued overseer of road in 1785.

WILLIAM SLADE (OF JOSAIS) continued overseer of road in 1785. [Note: Although it appears he was reappointed in 1786, the entry is crossed out of the minute book].

JAMES GITTINGS continued overseer of road in 1785-1786.

SAMUEL NORWOOD continued overseer of road in 1785-1786.

GABRIEL P. VANHORN appointed instead of David Poe to oversee road in 1785, and reappointed in 1786.

MICHAEL SNIDER appointed overseer of road laid out by Andrew Buchanan, Edward Cockey and Nathan Cromwell, beginning at a blazed red oak and white oak near a branch that descends from Samuel Worthington's field near where Benjamin Bond now lives, in a direct line along the stoney ridge in Charles Walker's field to a white oak at the corner of Thomas Matthews' field, and so on between the dwelling house and a mill, as laid out by aforesaid Commissioners, until it intersects the great road near the Dutch Church - 1785.

GEORGE HAILE, JR. appointed instead of John Hopkins to oversee road in 1786.

JONATHAN TIPTON, SR. appointed instead of Joseph Stansbury to oversee road in 1786.

THOMAS BENNETT appointed instead of Francis Snowden to oversee road in 1786.

JOHN GILLIS appointed instead of John Evans to oversee road in 1786.

WALTER DALLIS continued overseer of road in 1786.

WILLIAM STENSON continued overseer of road in 1786.

GABRIEL P. VANHORN continued overseer of road in 1786.

JAMES RICE appointed instead of John Barrow, Jr. to oversee road in 1786.

JOHN HASSELBACK appointed instead of George Beam to oversee road in 1786.

THOMAS RUTTER appointed instead of Thomas Harvey to oversee road in 1786.

SHADRACK GREEN appointed instead of John Standiford (of Jno.) to oversee road in 1786.

MICHAEL SNIDER continued overseer of road in 1786.

GREENBERRY WYLEY appointed overseer of road from William Slade's to William Gwinn's Mill dam, and from John Shepherd's lane to Cox's Ford on the Great Falls, and from thence until it intersects the main road leading from Wheeler's Mill to Charles Gorsuch's - 1786.

WILLIAM WYLEY appointed overseer of road from the south end of Miss Rachael Goodwin's lane on York Road to the line of Harford County, and from the north end of said lane to Daniel Shaw's, and from York Road to Little Falls of the Gunpowder through James Mc. Boyce's plantation - 1786.

DANIEL SHAW appointed overseer of road from York Road at Dimmitt's Lane to the west side of Gillis' Bridge, and from said road by Daniel Shaw's until it intersects the road leading from Mr. Slade's to William Gwinn's Mill - 1786.

JOHN TALBOTT appointed overseer of road from Gillis' Bridge to Curfman's Mill, and from thence to York Road in the fork of the Great Falls of the Gunpowder near Jacob Marshall's - 1786.

JOSEPH STANSBURY appointed overseer of road from Western Run at Ensor's to the upper side of Benjamin Rogers' Quarters - 1786.

WILLIAM DEMMETT appointed overseer from Little falls of Gunpowder to Mr. Dean's Run and from Little Falls to the Long Calm and from Mr. Dean's to Long Calm - April, 1790, and reappointed August, 1791, and June, 1792, and April, 1793.

JOHN HOPKINS appointed overseer from David Armstrong's down to Baltimore Town Upper Bridge and from Baltimore Town to Jonathan Hanson, Sr.'s Upper Mills and from thence until it intersects the main road below Job Garrettson's and from the main road by Richard Hopkins' through Charles Rogers plantation at Jones's Falls at John Stevenson's - April, 1790; not reappointed in 1791; reappointed June, 1792, and April, 1793.

MORDECAI PRICE (OF MORDECAI) appointed overseer from John Green's to Capt. Joshua Hall's Mill, from thence by Benjamin Hooker's, leaving said Hooker's house on the right hand until it intersects the road near Benjamin Wheeler's fence and from thence by John Clossey's until he comes as far as Nicholas Merryman's fence - April, 1790, and reappointed August, 1791, and June, 1792, and April, 1793.

GREENBERRY WHEELER appointed overseer from Benjamin Rogers' Quarter by Jonathan Tipton's across the Barrens to Anthony Null's as laid out by said Jonathan Tipton and Robert Lemmon - April, 1790.

NICODEMUS BOND appointed overseer from Stephen Gill's to the bottom of the large hill near Ledger's - April, 1790, and reappointed August, 1791, and June, 1792, and April, 1793.

WILLIAM TREMBLE appointed overseer from the Upper Bridge leading by Benjamin Rogers' meadow until it intersects the road from Philpott's Bridge to the Herring Run and the road from Fell's Point until it intersects the York Road leading to Baltimore Town - April, 1790.

JAMES CROW appointed overseer from Christopher Sewell's to Ely Dorsey's plantation and also the road from said Sewell's to Pontany's Mill and the Delaware Bottom Road - April, 1790, and reappointed August, 1791.

ELIAS DORSEY appointed overseer from Ely Dorsey's plantation to Frederick County - April, 1790.

CHARLES GORSUCH (OF CHARLES) appointed overseer of all roads from Wheeler's Mill, the main road leading to John Merryman's, and from thence to the Great Falls on Gunpowder that leads to York County - April, 1790.

JOHN GRIFFITH appointed overseer from the falls near Matthews' Mill until it intersects the public road near Daniel Bower's, and also from John Risteau's to Hudson's Mill - April, 1790, and reappointed August, 1791.

CHARLES ROBINSON appointed overseer from William Cromwell's Bridge on Gunpowder Great Falls to the road leading to Larsh's Mill until it intersects the main road in Baltimore Town that comes by Towson's from the new ford on the said falls until it intersects the said road and likewise from the ford on said falls at Richardson's until it intersects the road which leads to Larshes Bridge and the Old Court Road from Towson's to the Long Calm - April, 1790.

WALTER DOLLIS appointed overseer from John Mercer Porter's to "T", from the head of Middle River to intersect the main road that leads from said Porter's to "T" from the head of Middle River to intersect the main road that leads from aforesaid Porter's to "T" at the Widow Fowler's - April, 1790, and reappointed August, 1791, and June, 1792.

JAMES CAMPBELL appointed overseer of all public roads from the Great Falls on Gunpowder to York County - April, 1790.

GEORGE GOULDSMITH PRESBURY, JR. appointed overseer from "P" Hill to Nottingham Furnace, from Nathan Nicholson's to intersect the main road that leads from "P" Hill to the Nottingham Furnace, from said Nicholson's to the head of Middle River, and from Mr. Andrews' Gate to Frog Morton - April, 1790, and reappointed August, 1791, and June, 1792, and April, 1793.

MARTIN JUDY appointed overseer from the road above William Lux's leading to Mayberry Helms' and to Stephen Wooden's and from thence until it intersects the main road by John Price's - April, 1790, and reappointed August, 1791, and June, 1792, and April, 1793.

WILLIAM PRICE appointed overseer from Western Run near Dennis Garrett Coal's to Stephen Price's, from thence until it intersects the public road from Wheeler's Mill to Baltimore Town, from the Western Run near George Ensor's to Stephen Price's, and from Thomas Kitten's Saw Mill to the Quaker Meeting House, and from Kitten's Saw Mill until it intersects Benjamin Rogers' road by Benjamin Wheeler's plantation formerly called Hamilton - April, 1790, and reappointed August, 1791, and June, 1792, and April, 1793.

GREENBERRY BARTON appointed overseer from "T" to Baltimore Town - April, 1790.

JAMES WEBSTER appointed from "T" to Lee's Ford - April, 1790, and reappointed August, 1791, and June, 1792, and April, 1793.

DIXON STANSBURY, JR. appointed overseer from Slaid's Tavern to the main road to Benjamin Boyce's and from Josias Slaid's to Zachariah Strawble's Mills on the Little Falls Gunpowder that was laid out by Thomas Talbott and

Josias Slaid to open and clear and from Slaid's to the Little Falls by John Parker's - April, 1790, and reappointed August, 1791, and June, 1792, and April, 1793.

JOSEPH SUTTON appointed overseer from the temporary line until it intersects the Harford County line - April, 1790, and reappointed August, 1791, and June, 1792, and April, 1793.

AMON BUTLER, JR. appointed overseer of the main road from Josephus Murray's to George Myers' - April, 1790, and reappointed August, 1791, and June, 1792, and April, 1793.

JOHN ELLICOTT appointed overseer of the public roads from Welches Forge along the Hunting Ridge Road to Hood's Mill, also from Miller's until it intersects the road from Hood's Mill, the new road to Ellicott's Mill until it intersects the main road from Hood's Mill to Baltimore Town, and also the new road to Hood's Mill - April, 1790, and reappointed August, 1791, and June, 1792.

JAMES RICE appointed overseer of the public roads from Rebecca Claggett's to Dean's Run and from Rebecca Claggett's, Roger Boyce's and Abraham Jarrett's Mill ford to Jeremiah Chance's, and from said ford to William Standeford's - April, 1790, and reappointed August, 1791, and June, 1792, and April, 1793.

SAMUEL CHENOWETH appointed overseer from Winchester Town to Matthews' Mill - April, 1790, and reappointed August, 1791, and June, 1792, and April, 1793.

PATRICK LYNCH appointed overseer from the lower part of Patapsco Neck to the main road leading from Baltimore Town to Joppa, and from the fork of the road by Swann Harbour to the Herring Run - April, 1790, and reappointed August, 1791, and June, 1792, and April, 1793.

GEORGE BEAMS appointed overseer from Baltimore Town to the Garrison Church - April, 1790, and reappointed August, 1791, and June, 1792.

NATHAN WHEELER appointed overseer from Benjamin Rogers' Mill to the Western Run at Wheeler's Mill and from thence to the head of Mrs. Buchanan's lane - April, 1790.

JOHN WILMOTT (OF JOHN) appointed overseer on the York Road from the head of Mrs. Buchanan's lane to Towson's Tavern - April, 1790, and reappointed August, 1791, and June, 1792, and April, 1793.

SOLOMON ALLEN appointed overseer from the Conewago Road by John Read's plantation over Gwin's Falls by Howe's Mill to the Widow Owings' and from thence to Pontaney's Mill - April, 1790, and reappointed August, 1791.

JOHN CHAMBERLAIN appointed overseer from Boyce's to Mr. Dulany's ford on the Great Falls and from Boyce's to Mr. Gittings' Mill and from thence until it intersects the main road to Joppa, and from the Little Falls at the Rock Ford along the new road to the Great Falls, and from Francis Croskery's to Cromwell's Bridge - April, 1790, and reappointed August, 1791, and June, 1792, and April, 1793.

SAMUEL HUNT appointed overseer from the bottom of a hill near Ledger until it intersects the main road below Richard Hopkins', from Walter Smith's until it intersects the road near Ezekiel Towson's and from John Pitts' to the Garrison Church - April, 1790.

LEWIS PITTS appointed overseer from John Price's to the line between him and George Risteau's plantation across Aquila Price's land until it intersects the line between Mrs. Philpott's plantation and John Giles' Run then on the line between Jeremiah Johnson's and Stephen Gill's (son of John) until it comes to the plantation of John Price, Jr. - April, 1790, and reappointed August, 1791, and June, 1792, and April, 1793.

THOMAS RISTEAU appointed overseer from Samuel Owings' Gate near the bridge until it intersects the main road near Isgrigs Smith's shop, from Cookson's along the Old Court Road near Walter Smith's, and from Monk's Mill through the Pimlico until it intersects the public road - April, 1790, and reappointed August, 1791, and June, 1792, and April, 1793.

AMON BUTLER, SR. appointed overseer from St. Thomas' Church to Josephus Murray's - April, 1790, and reappointed August, 1791, and June, 1792, and April, 1793.

PETER KETHEIR appointed overseer of the main road leading from George Myers' to the Province Line towards Hanover Town - April, 1790, and reappointed August, 1791, and June, 1792, and April, 1793.

WALTER BOSLEY appointed overseer of the roads from David Armstrong's to Walter Dulany's ford on the Great Falls Gunpowder, from the place called Overshot Ford on Gunpowder Falls to the road leading from David Armstrong's to Walter Dulany's ford on the Great Falls - April, 1790, and reappointed August, 1791, and June, 1792. Walter was reappointed overseer of road only from David Armstrong's to Walter Dulaney's ford on the Great Falls of Gunpowder in April, 1793.

SHADRACK GREEN appointed overseer from Benjamin Rogers' Mill to Slaid's Tavern and from the roads at Burk's Old Field leading by Skelton Standiford's until it comes to Benjamin Boyce's - April, 1790, and reappointed August, 1791, and June, 1792, and April, 1793.

JAMES GITTINGS (OF THOMAS) appointed overseer from the Little Falls where Bond's Stave Road has its beginning, from thence through the land of Samuel Young and Charles Baker, Sr., nearly with a road sometime ago laid out through the said lands to the main road commonly called the Fork Road, from thence to cross the said road near a field of Mr. George Thornton's and then with a road through his and Mr. Charles Wells' land which has been commonly used for some years past to James Bosley's land and through a valley of Mr. Bosley's land near his fence to the house of Mr. Tredway's, and from thence with a road now commonly used to Thomas Lucas' Mill, then with the mill road from the said mill to the land of Capt. Charles Ridgely's, thence with his fence to the dwelling house of Henry Hendon and from Hendon's house with an old road to the Great Falls and from the Great Falls with a road that intersects the road below Peter Miles' at a place commonly known by the name of the White Oak Swamp - April, 1790, and reappointed August, 1791, and June, 1792, and April, 1793.

SAMUEL NORWOOD appointed overseer from the New Bridge across Gwin's Falls to Lawrence Hammond's Ferry and from the said bridge to the Main Falls of Patapsco by Robert Long's plantation - April, 1790, and reappointed August, 1791, and June, 1792, and April, 1793.

HENRY STOUFFER appointed overseer from the west side of Calvert Street in Baltimore Town to the Ferry Point and also from said town to Carroll's Bridge and Welches Forge - April, 1790, and reappointed August, 1791, and June, 1792.

MICHAEL SNIDER appointed overseer of the road laid out by Andrew Buchanan, Edward Cockey and Nathan Cromwell, beginning for said road at a blazed red oak and white oak standing near a branch that descends Samuel Worthington's field near where Benjamin Bond now lives, then with a direct line along the Stoney Ridge in Charles Walker's field to a white oak at the corner of Thomas Matthews' field and so on between the dwelling house and mill as laid out by the foresaid Commissioners and particularly expressed by them in their return until it intersects the Great Road near the Dutch Church - April, 1790, and reappointed August, 1791.

GREENBERRY WYLEY appointed overseer from William Slade's to William Gwinn's Mill dam and from John Shepherd's lane to Cox's Ford on the Great Falls and from thence until it intersects the main road leading from Wheeler's Mill to Charles Gorsuch's - April, 1790, and reappointed August, 1791, and June, 1792, and April, 1793.

RICHARD SAMPSON appointed overseer from the south end of Miss Rachel Goodwin's lane on the York Road to the line of Harford County, and from the north end of said lane to Daniel Shaw's and from the said York Road to the Little Falls of Gunpowder through James McBoyce's plantation - April, 1790.

DANIEL SHAW appointed overseer from the York Road at Demmitt's lane to the west side of Gillis' Bridge and from said road by Daniel Shaw's to intersect the road leading from Mr. Slaid's to William Gwinn's Mill - April, 1790, and reappointed August, 1791, and June, 1792, and April, 1793.

JOHN TALBOTT appointed overseer from Gillis' Bridge to Curfman's Mill and from thence to the York Road in the fork of the Great Falls of Gunpowder near Jacob Marshall's - April, 1790, and reappointed August, 1791, and June, 1792, and April, 1793.

RICHARD JOHNS appointed overseer from the Western Run at Ensor's to the upper side of Benjamin Rogers' Quarter - April, 1790, and reappointed August, 1791, and June, 1792, and April, 1793.

JOHN JACOBS appointed overseer from Westminster Town to Peter Goslin's - April, 1790, and reappointed August, 1791, and June, 1792, and April, 1793.

WILLIAM BEASMAN appointed overseer from Peter Goslin's to Nicholas Jones' and from Peter Goslin's to John Moale's Quarter - April, 1790, and reappointed August, 1791, and June, 1792, and April, 1793.

WILLIAM MATTHEWS (Gunpowder) appointed overseer from the York Road near John Davis' until it intersects the county road near Daniel McComiskey's - April, 1790, and reappointed August, 1791, and June, 1792, and April, 1793.

GEORGE STORM appointed overseer from the Black Rock Mills and running on the west side of said mill dam until it intersects the land of Mordecai Cole, thence through the sais Cole's lands leaving the late dwelling house of Barney Ford on the left, thence to the foot of a ridge of land the property of John Hare, thence keeping the said ridge until it intersects the lands of Robert Caple, thence through the said Caple's woodland until it intersects the dividing line between John Busby and Matthias Wiesner, thence with a straight line until it intersects the land of Thomas Gent, then through said Gent's land leaving his apple orchard on the north until it intersects the land of Joseph Shaul, thence down on Barren Ridge to the foot of a meadow the property of David Stoddard, thence crossing the said meadow and taking the first ridge on the north side (being the dividing ridge between the drafts of Piney Run and Gunpowder Falls) and keeping the said ridge until it intersects the Connowago Road - April, 1790.

CHRISTIAN GORE appointed overseer from Worthington's Mill until it intersects the main road near Josephus Murray's and from said mill until it intersects the main road near Francis Wells' - April, 1790, and reappointed August, 1791, and June, 1792, and August, 1793.

NATHANIEL STINCHCOMB, SR. appointed overseer from Johannes Miller's to the falls of Patapsco at Mr. Hamilton's - April, 1790, and reappointed August, 1791, and June, 1792, and April, 1793.

ROBERT LYON appointed overseer from Jones' Quarter to Dr. Lyons' Mill, from the mill to the main road, and from said Jones' Quarter to the Garrison Church - April, 1790, and reappointed August, 1791, and June, 1792, and April, 1793.

CONROD CARLINGER appointed overseer from George Myers' to the Province Line leading to York - April, 1790, and reappointed August, 1791, and June, 1792, and April, 1793.

JOSIAS BOWER replaced William Demmitt as overseer - August, 1791.

BRYAN TIPTON replaced Greenberry Wheeler as overseer - August, 1791, and reappointed June, 1792, and April, 1793.

FRANCIS DAWS replaced William Tremble as overseer - August, 1791.

BENJAMIN LAWRENCE replaced Elias Dorsey as overseer - August, 1791, and reappointed June, 1792, and April, 1793.

DAVID SMITHSON replaced Charles Robinson as overseer - August, 1791, and reappointed June, 1792, and April, 1793.

BENJAMIN DAVIS replaced James Campbell as overseer - August, 1791, and reappointed June, 1792, and April, 1793.

BENJAMIN GASH replaced Greenberry Barton as overseer - August, 1791.

WILLIAM PERRIGOE replaced Nathan Wheeler as overseer - August, 1791.

JOHN COCKEY (OF THOMAS) replaced Samuel Hunt as overseer - August, 1791, and reappointed June, 1792, and April, 1793.

NICHOLAS HUTCHINS, JR. replaced Richard Sampson as overseer - August, 1791, and reappointed June, 1792, and April, 1793.

MORDECAI WHEELER replaced George Storm as overseer - August, 1791, and reappointed June, 1792, and April, 1793.

JAMES BROWN appointed overseer of the public road from the Upper Bridge in Baltimore Town to Jonathan Hanson, Sr.'s Upper Mill - October, 1791, and reappointed June, 1792.

JAMES EDWARDS replaced Francis Daws as overseer - June, 1792, and April, 1793.

JOHN GLOVER replaced James Crow as overseer - June, 1792, and reappointed April, 1793.

DICKENSON GORSUCH replaced Nathan Wheeler as overseer - June, 1792, and reappointed April, 1793.

NATHAN CHAPMAN replaced John Griffith as overseer - June, 1792, and reappointed April, 1793.

JOHN BATTEE replaced Benjamin Gash as overseer - June, 1792.

JOHN TULLY YOUNG replaced William Perrigoe as overseer - June, 1792, and reappointed April, 1793.

WILLIAM COOPER replaced Solomon Allen as overseer - June, 1792, and reappointed April, 1793.

GEORGE TANNER replaced Michael Snider as oversee - June, 1792, and reappointed April, 1793.

GEORGE CHILDS appointed overseer of the hew road laid out agreeable to Act of Assembly passed November session 1791 from Ellicott's Mill seat on Jones' Falls to or near the east corner of the poor house land - June, 1791, and reappointed April, 1793.

JOSHUA TIPTON appointed overseer of the public road from John Price's to continue along the old road until it intersects the beaver dams at the old fording place and from thence up the Spring Branch of Joshua Jones' where a foot and horse road now is and to go by the barn and through the plantation of the said Joshua Jones until it intersects the main road by Mr. John Cockey's lime kiln - June, 1792, and reappointed April, 1793.

CHARLES JESSOP appointed overseer on the Old Court Road from Towson's to the Long Calm - April, 1793.

ROBERT PORTER replaced Walter Dollis as overseer - April, 1793.

ELISHA SOLLERS replaced John Battee as overseer - April, 1793.

SOLOMON WOODEN replaced John Ellicott as overseer - April, 1793.

RICHARD BRITTAIN appointed overseer from the Overshot Ford on Gunpowder Falls until it intersects the road leading from Towson's Tavern to Walter Dulaney's ford - April, 1793.

HENRY NAUGLE appointed overseer from the west side of Calvert Street in Baltimore Town to the Ferry Point and also from said town to Carroll's Bridge and Welches Forge - April, 1793. [Note: In the minute book the name of Henry Stouffer was entered, but the surname Stouffer was lined out and the surname Naugle was written in over it].

WILLIAM LYNCH appointed overseer of the new laid out road by Thomas Todd and James Baker from Baltimore Town to the White Marsh Run, agreeable to the Act of Assembly passed November 1791 session - April, 1793.

JOHN PAUL appointed overseer of the new laid out road by Thomas Todd and James Baker from the White Marsh Run to the Little Falls of Gunpowder, agreeable to the Act of Assembly passed November 1791 session - April, 1793.

INDEX

-A-

ADAIR, Robert, 38, 39
ADAMS, Henry, 61, 65
ALEXANDER, Mark, 82
ALLEN,
  Joseph, 11
  Solomon, 89, 93, 99, 104
ALLENDER,
  Joseph, 92
  William, 92, 93
AMOS,
  Benjamin, 40, 47, 52, 57, 61, 65, 68, 74
  William, 16, 20, 24, 31, 65, 68
AMOSS, William, 72
ANDERSON,
  Benjamin, 25
  Daniel, 43, 78
  John, 15, 19
ANDREW, William, 16, 20, 24, 37, 40, 52, 64, 68, 72, 75, 84, 87
ANDREWS,
  Dr., 78
  Ephraim, 43
  Mr., 98
  William, 31, 32, 38, 46, 52, 56, 60, 94
ARCHER,
  James, 43
  Thomas, 25, 51, 56, 60, 64
ARDEN, Samuel, 3
ARMSTRONG,
  David, 73, 76, 78, 79, 83, 84, 85, 86, 89, 90, 91, 97, 100
  John, 2, 3
ARNOLD, Joseph, 37
ASHMAN,
  George, 29, 35
  John, 4
ASHMORE, William, 14, 18, 22, 67, 71

-B-

BACON, John, 85, 87, 89, 92, 93
BAILEY,
  George, 7
  John, 31, 35
  McClain, 55
  McLain, 60, 64, 67
  McLane, 40, 50
BAILY, McLane, 44
BAKER,
  Charles, 17, 41, 47, 53, 57, 62, 66, 69, 81, 84, 101
  James, 76, 104
  Morris, 16, 20, 27, 38, 73
  Zebediah, 7
BALE, Anthony, 2, 3
BANKSON, Joseph, 65, 68
BARNEY,
  Absalom, 13, 16, 20, 24, 39, 40, 42, 47, 48, 52, 53, 57, 58, 65, 69, 70, 73, 74, 79, 84
  Absolom, 61
  John, 79
  William, 35
BARROW, John, 87, 89, 92, 95, 96
BARTON, Greenberry, 98, 103
BATTEE, John, 104
BAXTER, William, 47, 57
BAY, William, 73
BEAM, George, 95, 96
BEAMS, George, 99
BEASMAN,
  Joseph, 29
  William, 101
BECK,
  Mathew, 37
  Matthew, 34
BEECH, Henry, 38
BELT, John, 7, 13, 17, 21
BENNENTON, Henry, 21
BENNETT,
  Thomas, 96
  William, 22, 24, 40, 44, 46, 50, 51, 55, 56, 59, 60, 63, 64, 68, 71
BIDDISON,
  Jarvis, 24, 46, 52
  Jere., 16, 46, 52
  Jervis, 16, 20, 40, 56, 60, 64, 68, 72
  Thomas, 16, 20
BILLINGSLEY, James, 38, 61, 65, 73
BISHOP, Robert, 57
BODY, Stephen, 11
BOND,
  Beale, 40
  Benjamin, 17, 21, 31, 32, 96, 101
  Daniel, 27, 73
  Jacob, 39, 44, 50, 55
  John, 15, 19, 23, 27, 45, 51, 64, 68, 72, 74
  Joshua, 15, 19, 23, 59, 63, 67, 71
  Nicodemus, 97
  Peter, 4
  Richard, 36
  Thomas, 3, 14, 15, 18, 19, 20, 22, 23, 25, 27, 30, 31, 33, 35, 40, 44, 45, 50, 51, 55, 59, 63, 64, 65, 67, 69, 71, 73
  Widow, 32
  William, 2, 3, 6, 8
BOON, Thomas, 33
BOONE, Nicholas, 23
BOOTHBY, Edward, 1
BORDLEY, Mr., 63
BOREING, John, 39, 43, 49, 54, 63
BORING, John, 59
BOSLEY,
  James, 81, 84, 101
  Walter, 3, 90, 93, 95, 100
  William, 22
BOTTS, George, 16, 20, 72
BOWEN,
  Benjamin, 9, 13, 18, 22, 26, 29, 35, 36, 39, 42, 48, 54, 58, 62, 66, 70, 83, 93, 95
  John, 13, 24
  Josias, 52, 56, 60, 76, 80, 83, 85, 87, 89, 92
  Nathan, 37
  Reece, 33
  Solomon, 86, 88, 90

INDEX

BOWER,
  Daniel, 98
  Josias, 103
BOWSER, Daniel,
  74, 79, 82,
  84, 87
BOYCE,
  Benjamin, 80,
    81, 91, 98,
    100
  James Mc., 96
  Mr., 16, 20,
    41, 47, 61,
    65, 69, 73,
    77, 78, 81,
    83, 86, 88,
    90, 93
  Roger, 17, 25,
    27, 38, 39,
    41, 43, 44,
    47, 49, 53,
    54, 55, 57,
    59, 62, 69,
    76, 80, 85,
    87, 99
BOYD, Abraham, 32
BOZEMAN, William,
  23
BOZLEY,
  Jo., 17, 61, 65
  John, 54, 58,
    62
  Joseph, 59, 63
  William, 14,
    18, 62, 67,
    70
BRADFORD,
  Capt., 37
  William, 6, 28
BRADY, Cornelius,
  43, 49
BREREWOOD,
  Mr., 29
  Thomas, 28
BRIAN, Js., 58
BRICE, Samuel, 33
BRIERLY, Robert,
  21
BRITTAIN,
  Abraham, 79,
    82, 84, 87,
    91
  Abram, 88
  Nicholas, 91,
    92, 94
  Richard, 104
BROAD,
  John, 1
  Thomas, 8, 12
BROWN,
  Abel, 21, 66,
    69, 84, 87,
    88, 91
  George, 17, 36
  James, 103
  John, 2, 3, 21, 22
BRYAN, James, 73,
  79, 82
BRYERLY, Robert, 74
BUCHANAN,
  ---, 11
  Andrew, 14, 18,
    71, 96, 101
  Archibald, 26
  George, 8
  Mrs., 99
  Widow, 15, 23, 44,
    50
  William, 18
BUCK,
  Benjamin, 85, 87
  John, 2, 16, 20,
    24, 72, 75, 80,
    82, 92
BUCKLE, Joseph, 43
BUCKLEY,
  Jo., 14, 18, 63,
    67, 71
  Joseph, 20, 22,
    39, 43, 49, 54,
    59
BUCKNER, William, 7
BULL,
  Abraham, 57, 60
  Abrm., 52
  Edward, 21, 25
  Jacob, 15, 36, 47,
    52, 57, 60, 65,
    73, 74
  John, 40, 47, 52,
    57
BURCHFIELD, Thomas,
  6, 8, 9
BURNEY, William, 7
BUSBY, John, 101
BUSSEY,
  Bennett, 83, 85
  Jesse, 80
BUTLER,
  Absalom, 13, 48,
    53, 57, 62, 70
  Amon, 85, 87, 88,
    89, 90, 92, 94,
    95, 99, 100
  Henry, 2, 3, 5, 7,
    10
  Widow, 13, 15, 19,
    21, 23, 42, 44,
    48, 50, 53, 55,
    57, 62, 63, 66,
    70
BUTTERWORTH,
  Joseph, 34
  Widow, 28

-C-
CADLE, Benjamin, 10,
  11
CAIN, James, 34, 64,
  68, 72
CAINE, James, 37
CALDER, James, 23
CAMPBELL,
  James, 88, 92, 94,
    98, 103
  John, 35
CANNON, Thomas, 3
CAPLE, Robert, 101
CAREY, James, 59, 63
CARLINGER, Conrod,
  103
CARLISLE, Peter, 23
CARMAN, John, 27
CARNAN, Christopher,
  23
CARR,
  Aquila, 49, 54
  Thomas, 77, 86
  Widow, 17, 25
CARROL, Peter, 11
CARROLL,
  Charles, 30
  Dr., 44, 50, 55
  Peter, 38
CARTER, John, 3
CHALK, John, 20
CHAMBERLAIN, John,
  36, 38, 49, 54,
  59, 63, 94, 95,
  100
CHAMIER, Mr., 26
CHAMNBERLAIN, John,
  43
CHANCE, Jeremiah, 76,
  85, 87, 99
CHANCY, George, 2
CHANEY, Benjamin
  Burgess, 21
CHAPMAN,
  ---, 11
  Jonathan, 34
  Nathan, 103
  Robert, 29
CHAULK, John, 24
CHAUNCY, George, 2
CHENOWETH,
  Arthur, 79
  John, 79
  Samuel, 85, 99
CHENOWITH, Samuel,
  87, 89, 92, 95
CHEYNE, Roderick, 17,
  42, 53, 58, 62
CHEYNES, Roderick, 48
CHILCOAT, John, 17,
  25
CHILDS, George, 104

INDEX

CHINOITH,
  Richard, 46, 52
CHITWYND,
  William, 34
CHRITARD, John, 15, 19, 23, 72
CLAGGET, Rebecca, 76, 80, 85, 87
CLAGGETT,
  Rebecca, 99
CLARK,
  John, 15, 19, 23, 68, 72
  Law., 45, 51, 64
  Lawrance, 15, 19, 22, 23, 44, 59, 63, 71
  Lawrence, 19, 50, 55, 72
  Robert, 32
  William, 61, 63, 65, 69, 73
CLOSSEY, John, 74, 79, 82, 84, 86, 90, 97
COAL, Dennis
  Garrett, 98
COALE, Skipwith, 12, 29, 30
COCKEY,
  Edward, 77, 81, 90, 93, 96, 101
  John, 77, 81, 94, 95, 103, 104
  Joshua, 4
  Thomas, 103
COLE,
  Christopher, 13, 39, 42, 48, 53, 58, 70
  Dennis, 13, 33, 39, 42, 48, 53, 58, 70
  Dennis Garrett, 36, 75, 80, 89, 91
  Mordecai, 101
  Philip, 16, 19
  Skipwith, 16
  Thomas, 30, 75
  William, 13, 18, 86, 88, 90
COLEGATE,
  Benjamin, 22, 32, 44, 50, 55, 59, 63, 71
  John, 38, 63, 67
COLLESON, William, 3
COLLYDAY, Jacob, 15, 19, 71
COOK,
  John, 15, 72
  William, 6
COOKE, William, 4
COOKSON, Samuel, 26, 76
COOPER, William, 104
COPELAND, William, 36
CORD,
  Abraham, 11
  Thomas, 1
COS, William, 54
COWEN, John, 29
COX,
  Jacob, 27
  John, 27
  William, 22, 43, 45, 49, 58, 62, 67, 70, 78
CRABTREE, Thomas, 45, 51
CRISSAP, Thomas, 12
CRITCHARD, John, 45, 51, 64
CRITCHET, John, 41, 43, 45, 49
CROCKETT, Gilbert, 10
CROKER, Thomas, 2
CROMWELL,
  Joseph, 40, 44, 50, 55, 81, 83, 86
  Mr., 26
  Nathan, 96, 101
  Oliver, 12
  Stephen, 86, 88
  Thomas, 3
  William, 75, 77, 79, 81, 83, 86, 88, 90, 91, 93, 98
CROSKERY, Francis, 100
CROSS,
  Henry, 13, 16, 20, 21, 61, 65, 69, 70, 73
  John, 13, 18, 42, 48, 53, 58, 62, 66, 70
  Thomas, 10

CROW, James, 97, 103
CROXALL,
  Charles, 15, 19, 23, 40, 44, 50, 55, 60, 64, 67, 71
  Richard, 38
CROXWELL, Mr., 26
CULLIN, Thomas, 9
CULLINGS, Thomas, 8
CULVER, Benjamin, 43, 45, 62, 64, 67
CURTIS, Daniel, 81, 83

-D-

DALLAM,
  Josias William, 78
  William, 29, 30
DALLAS, Walter, 30
DALLIS, Walter, 94, 96
DAUGHADAY, John, 17, 25
DAUGHERDY, John, 25
DAUGHERTY, John, 77, 81, 83, 86
DAVIS,
  Benjamin, 103
  Henry, 21
  Jacob, 14, 18, 44, 50, 55
  John, 101
  Richard, 13, 17
  Uriah, 17, 61, 65
DAWS,
  Francis, 103
  Isaac, 20
DAY,
  Edward, 31, 35, 58, 62
  John, 14, 18, 22, 59, 63, 67, 70
  Nicholas, 7, 8, 10, 12
  Samuel, 39, 41, 74
DEAN,
  Mr., 14, 17, 18, 22, 41, 44, 47, 50, 53, 55, 57, 59, 63, 69, 71, 73, 76, 78, 80, 84, 85, 87, 97
DEAVER,
  Antill, 15, 19, 23, 45, 51, 64, 72
  John, 9, 74, 79, 82, 84, 87, 91
  Richard, 45, 51, 56, 60
DEAVOR,
  John, 28

INDEX

Richard, 40
DEBRULAR,
  William, 14, 70
DECKER,
  Frederick, 77
DEMMETT, William, 97
DEMMIT, John, 13, 17, 42, 53
DEMMITT,
  James, 77
  John, 48
  William, 94, 103
DENBO, John, 20, 24
DENTON, William, 1
DIMMITT, John, 80, 82, 85
DOLLIS, Walter, 98, 104
DONNAHUE, Henry, 2
DORSEY,
  Edward, 13, 17, 21, 69
  Elias, 97, 103
  Elisha, 79, 82
  Ely, 79, 84, 91, 97
  Nicholas, 27, 36, 41, 47, 53, 57, 61, 66, 69, 74
DRAPER, Lawrence, 3
DREW,
  Anthony, 1
  George, 5, 6
DRISDEL, Robert, 1
DSEMMITT,
  William, 93
DUKE,
  Christopher, 11
DULANEY,
  Esquire, 7
  Mr., 86
  Walter, 104
DULANY,
  Mr., 77, 83, 88, 90, 100
  Walter, 78, 83, 90, 100
DUNN,
  John, 57
  Robert, 24
DURBIN,
  Daniel, 42, 48

  John, 6
  Samuel, 8
  Thomas, 40, 47, 52, 57
DURHAM,
  James, 3
  Samuel, 15
DURKIN, Michael, 73
DURKINS, Michael, 69
DUSKIN, Michael, 73
DUSKINS, Michael, 69

-E-

EAGER, John, 4
EAGLESTON, Abraham, 46, 52, 56, 60
EDWARDS, James, 103
ELDER, John, 79, 82
ELICOTT, John, 104
ELLET, George, 20
ELLICOTT, John, 93, 95, 99
ELLIDGE, Joseph, 29
ELLIOTT,
  George, 16, 39, 41, 47, 61, 65, 69, 73
  Thomas, 39, 41
ENSOR,
  Abraham, 93
  George, 42, 48, 75, 79, 80, 82, 84, 86, 89, 90, 91, 92, 94, 98
  John, 7, 8, 93, 94
ETLE, Alexander, 43
ETTE, Alexander, 43
EVANS,
  Job, 18
  John, 41, 47, 79, 94, 96
EVERHART, George, 81, 83, 86, 88, 90

-F-

FARMER,
  Gregory, 31, 33
  John, 29, 32
FELL, Edward, 68, 72
FISHER, Michael, 18, 22, 94, 95
FITSIMONDS,
  Nicholas, 4
FITSREDMAN, John, 4
FLEMING, Robert, 22
FORD,
  Barney, 101
  Thomas, 33
FORREST, William, 3
FORSTER, John, 27
FORWARD, John, 55

FOSTER, John, 92, 94
FOWLER,
  James, 28
  Widow, 94, 98
  William, 21
FRANKLIN,
  Major, 46, 52
  T:, 39
  Thomas, 8, 12, 38, 93, 94
FREEMAN, Joseph, 5
FRIER, Bald, 61, 66
FRISBY, Perrigrin, 11

-G-

GALLION,
  James, 34, 45, 49
  John, 2, 5
GALLON, James, 45
GALLOWAY,
  Widow, 29
  William, 75, 79, 82
GARRET, Amos, 78
GARRETSON,
  Edward, 76, 78
  George, 9, 37
  James, 30, 37
GARRETT,
  Abraham, 27
  Amos, 46, 51
  Henry, 28, 34, 39, 44, 50
GARRETTSON,
  George, 10
  Job, 97
GARRISON, Job, 74, 79, 84, 86, 90
GASH, Benjamin, 103, 104
GASSAWAY, Thomas, 61, 66
GATES, John, 77, 81, 83
GAY,
  Nicholas Ruxton, 32
  Ruxton, 43, 49, 54, 59, 63
GENT, Thomas, 101
GEST, Thomas, 37
GIDDINGS, Thomas, 7, 8
GILBERT,
  Charles, 42, 48, 54, 58
  Gervis, 14, 42, 48, 67, 70
  Jervice, 54
  Jervis, 38, 58, 62
  Michael, 14, 34, 58, 70
GILES,
  Jacob, 9, 14, 18,

INDEX

22, 71
James, 78
John, 64, 68, 100
GILGRIST, Robert, 38
GILL,
  John, 3, 38, 74, 77, 79, 81, 82, 83, 84, 86, 88, 90, 93, 100
  Stephen, 5, 26, 36, 47, 52, 74, 77, 81, 87, 97, 100
GILLIS, John, 96
GILLS,
  John, 83
  Stephen, 83
GILVERT, Gervis, 58
GIST,
  Christopher, 11, 29, 33
  Joseph, 76
  Mr., 12, 30
  Nathaniel, 10
  Thomas, 23, 76, 80, 81, 83, 85, 88, 89
  William, 26, 38
GITTINGS,
  Asael, 13, 17, 21, 25, 69
  James, 83, 88, 90, 93, 95, 101
  Mr., 77, 83, 86, 90, 100
  Thomas, 39, 41, 43, 49, 59, 63, 81, 83, 88, 90, 101, 54
GLOVER, John, 103
GOODWIN,
  Lyde, 38
  Rachael, 96
  Rachel, 101
  Widow, 75
GOOSE, Adam, 66, 70
GORE, Christian, 101
GORSUCH,
  Charles, 9, 27, 74, 75, 79, 81, 82, 84, 94, 96, 97, 101
  Dickenson, 103

Loveless, 16, 20, 24, 40, 47, 52, 57, 60, 65, 68, 72
  Robert, 2
  Thomas, 5, 78, 81
  Widow, 16, 65, 68
  William, 17, 25
GOSLIN, Peter, 101
GOSNEL, Peter, 76
GOSNELL,
  John, 68, 72
  Peter, 15, 19, 23, 32, 33, 36, 68, 72, 80, 85, 89
GOTT, Richard, 6
GOVER,
  Ephraim, 24, 46, 51
  Philip, 23, 68, 72
GOZLIN, Peter, 26
GRAFTON, William, 16, 20, 25, 34, 36, 73
GREEN,
  Benjamin, 61, 65
  Henry, 21, 22, 44, 50, 55, 59, 63, 71
  John, 61, 65, 86, 97
  Shadrack, 96, 100
GREENIFF, John, 2
GREENWOOD, Thomas, 95
GRIFFIN,
  Luke, 49, 59, 63, 72
  Samuel, 15, 19, 25
GRIFFITH,
  John, 87, 88, 91, 92, 94, 95, 98, 103
  Luke, 14, 54, 67, 71
  Samuel, 24, 76
GROVER, George, 3
GUDGEON,
  Henry, 88, 90
  Sutton, 83, 86, 88, 90, 93
GWINN,
  William, 96, 101

-H-

HAIL, Neal, 70
HAILE,
  George, 96
  Neal, 17
  Nicholas, 34, 35, 36

HALL,
  Aquila, 6, 28
  Carvil, 77, 78
  Col., 14, 42, 46, 48, 51, 54, 58, 62, 67, 70
  Edward, 5, 6, 9, 11, 28, 78
  Esquire, 6, 8, 11
  John, 2, 4, 15, 19, 24, 25, 28, 40, 45, 51, 56, 60, 64, 68, 72, 74, 78
  Joshua, 74, 76, 84, 86, 97
  Parker, 31
  Widow, 45, 51, 64
  William, 10, 78
HAMBLETON, Mr., 19, 23, 68, 72
HAMILTON,
  John, 14, 30, 36, 39, 43, 49, 54, 59, 63, 67, 70
  Mr., 76, 81, 93, 103
  Mrs., 26
  William, 9, 11, 14, 18, 36, 43, 45, 49, 51, 54, 56
HAMMILTON, John, 33, 34
HAMMOND,
  Lawrance, 71
  Lawrence, 90, 101
  Morcecai, 82
  William, 8, 10, 12, 30, 77
HAMPTON, John, 40, 42
HANSON,
  John, 45, 51, 64, 72, 78
  Jonathan, 13, 21, 33, 42, 48, 53, 57, 62, 66, 70, 73, 79, 84, 86, 90, 97, 103
  Mary, 7
  Widow, 7
HARE, John, 101
HARRIMAN, John, 2
HARRIOTT, Oliver, 7, 10
HARRIS,
  Edward, 5
  John, 15, 19
  Loyd, 8
  Samuel, 51, 56, 60, 64
  Thomas, 7
HARRISON, Thomas, 23

INDEX

HARRYMAN,
  George, 12, 37
  John, 2, 38, 70
HARRYS, Loyd, 8
HARTIGIM,
  William, 26
HARVEY,
  Thomas, 83, 86,
    88, 90, 95,
    96
  William, 91,
    92, 94
HARWOOD, William,
  57
HASSELBACK, John,
  96
HAWKINS, John,
  26, 77
HELMS,
  George, 93, 94
  Mabry, 33
  Mayberry, 66,
    70, 89, 92,
    94, 98
  Maybury, 75
HENDON,
  Henry, 82, 84,
    101
  Josias, 7
HENLEY, Darby, 12
HERBERT,
  Benjamin, 78
HERNLY, Darby, 31
HERRYMAN, John,
  38
HICK, William, 21
HILL,
  Widow, 22
  William, 14,
    18, 59, 63,
    67, 71
HILLEN, John, 5
HINTON, Samuel, 4
HITCHCOCK,
  Asael, 56
  Asahel, 51
HOBBY, William,
  90, 93, 94
HOCSTON, Mr., 8
HOLLAND, Col., 8,
  12
HOLLINGSWORTH,
  Jesse, 74
HOOFMAN, William,
  85, 87, 88
HOOK, Jacob, 91,
  92, 95
HOOKER,
  Barney, 76, 80,
    83
  Benjamin, 86,
    88, 90, 92,
    97
  Thomas, 1
HOPKINS,
  John, 94, 96, 97
  Joseph, 29
  Nicholas, 91, 93
  Richard, 26, 37,
    77, 79, 83, 84,
    86, 88, 90, 97,
    100
  Samuel, 31, 39,
    42, 48, 54
  William, 15, 24,
    40, 46, 51, 56,
    60, 64, 68, 72
HORNE, William, 1
HORNER, Thomas, 31,
  41, 43, 49
HORTON, William, 14,
  18, 22, 67, 70
HORWARD, John, 20,
  21
HOWARD,
  Benjamin, 5
  Cornelius, 11, 19,
    23, 31, 44, 50,
    55, 63, 67, 71
  Cornelus, 37
  Henry, 91, 92
  John, 73, 78, 82
  John Greniff, 21
  Thomas, 88, 91, 93
  Thomas G., 84, 86
  William, 2
HOWELL, Samuel, 11,
  22
HUGHES, Samuel, 5
HUGHS,
  John, 15, 72
  Thomas, 4, 5
HUNT, Samuel, 88,
  90, 93, 94,
  100, 103
HURD, ---, 11
HUTCHINS,
  Nicholas, 12, 32,
    103
  Thomas, 2, 7, 8,
    36
HYDE, ---, 11

-I-
INGRAM,
  Arthur, 19, 51,
    56, 60, 64, 77
  Benjamin, 25
  Peazley, 30
ISHAM, James, 6
ISRAEL, John, 4

-J-
JACKS, Richard, 15,
  19
JACKSON,
  Philip, 65, 69
  Robert, 4
JACOBS, John, 101
JAMES, Henry, 61, 66
JARMAN, Widow, 34
JARRETT, Abraham, 47,
  52, 57, 60, 65,
  76, 80, 85, 87,
  99
JEFFERY, Robert, 43
JENKINS, Richard, 10
JESSOP, Charles, 104
JOHNS,
  Hosie, 68
  Hozier, 64
  Richard, 31, 40,
    45, 51, 56, 101
JOHNSON,
  Jeremiah, 13, 70,
    77, 81, 83, 100
  Richard, 41
  Thomas, 8, 12, 15,
    17, 19, 24, 34,
    41, 43, 46, 47,
    49, 51, 53, 54,
    57, 59, 63, 64,
    68, 69, 74
  William, 41, 47,
    61, 66
JONES,
  Benjamin, 29
  Capt., 11
  Evin, 15, 19, 23,
    67, 68, 71, 72
  Joshua, 104
  Nicholas, 76, 80,
    85, 89, 101
  Philip, 10, 40, 46,
    52, 56, 60
JUDY, Martin, 98

-K-
KANTWELL, Edward, 3
KEEN,
  Pollard, 45, 51,
    56, 60, 64
  Timothy, 43
KEENE, Pollard, 40
KELLEY, Thomas, 60
KELLY,
  Thomas, 20, 47, 52,
    57, 65, 72
  William, 80, 83,
    85, 87, 89, 91
KENNEDAY, Thomas, 43
KETHEIR, Peter, 100
KEY, Job, 74
KING, William, 11
KITELY, William, 14,
  39, 44, 47, 50,

INDEX

55, 71
KITTEN, Thomas, 75, 80, 89, 91, 98
KNIGHT, William, 34
KRANER, Michael, 93, 95

-L-

LANE,
 Dutton, 40, 42
 Thomas, 74, 85, 87, 89
LARSH, Valentine, 21, 49, 55, 69
LATHIM, John, 78
LAWRENCE,
 Benjamin, 84, 87, 88, 92, 94, 103
LAWSON,
 Mr., 16, 17, 42, 46, 48, 52, 53, 58, 62
LEE,
 Corbin, 15, 17, 21, 25, 64, 68, 72, 74
 James, 16, 19, 34, 68, 72
 Mr., 75, 76, 80, 85, 87
 Samuel, 15, 19, 64, 68, 72
LEGGETT, George, 93, 95
LEIGH, James, 34
LEMMON, Robert, 91, 97
LENOX, William, 1
LESTER, Peter, 3
LEWIS,
 ---, 11
 Edward, 43, 49, 55
 Joseph, 41, 47
 William, 37
LIDDICK, Peter, 94
LITTLE, George, 75
LITTON, Thomas, 8, 9
LLOYD, John, 30, 31
LONG,
 John, 30, 38
 Robert, 80, 90, 101

LOTWOOD, John, 1
LOVE, James, 43
LOW, John, 76, 80, 85, 89
LOWE, William, 12
LUCAS, Thomas, 82, 84, 101
LUX, William, 13, 21, 42, 48, 53, 57, 62, 66, 70, 75, 89, 98
LYALL, John, 14, 19, 23, 45, 51, 56, 64, 68, 70, 72
LYNCH,
 D., 17
 Patrick, 95, 99
 William, 104
LYON,
 Dr., 19, 76, 93
 John, 54, 58
 Robert, 103
 William, 39
LYONS, Dr., 15, 23, 26, 64, 81, 103
LYSTON, James, 87, 88, 91
LYTLE, Thomas, 60, 64
LYTTLEJOHN, Thomas, 47, 52, 57, 60, 65

-M-

MCBOYCE, James, 101
MCCABE, James, 43
MCCANDLESS, George, 73, 74
MCCOMAS, Aaron, 22
MACCOMAS, Alexander, 9, 55, 63
MCCOMAS,
 Alexander, 44, 50
 Daniel, 27
MACCOMAS, John, 63
MCCOMAS, William, 27
MCCOMISKEY, Daniel, 101
MACCOMUS,
 Alexander, 11, 67
 Daniel, 65, 69
 John, 59
 William, 65, 69
MCCUBBIN, William, 13, 17
MACCUBBIN,
 Zachariah, 26
MCCUBBIN, Zachariah, 75, 80, 83, 85, 87, 89
MCCULLOCK, David, 66, 69

MCDONOGH, John, 91, 92
MCGAW, Adam, 19
MACNEMARA, Michael, 29
MADOLE, Robert, 43
MAINER, William, 8
MARSH, Thomas, 49
MARSHALL, Jacob, 97, 101
MARTIN,
 Isaac, 43
 James, 43
 John, 43
MASH, Thomas, 54
MASSEY,
 Acquila, 29
 Aquila, 6, 9, 10
 Jonathan, 6
MATHERS, James, 14, 18
MATHEW, Thomas, 66, 70
MATHEWS,
 George, 48, 53, 58
 Henry, 9
 James, 14
 John, 15, 46, 51, 56, 60, 64, 68
 Mr., 8
 Roger, 2, 5, 6, 9, 28
 Thomas, 13, 17, 42, 44, 48, 50, 53, 55, 58, 62
MATTHEWS,
 John, 40, 72
 Thomas, 96, 101
 William, 101
MAXWELL, James, 27, 30
MAXWILL, James, 34
MECIN, William, 43
MERCER, John, 85, 87, 94
MEREDETH, Samuel, 43, 49, 54, 59, 63
MEREDITH,
 Samuel, 46, 52
 Thomas, 65
MERRYMAN,
 Benjamin, 74, 79, 82, 84, 87, 88, 92
 Charles, 29
 John, 27, 33, 41, 42, 48, 53, 70, 74, 79, 82, 92, 97
 Nicholas, 27, 42, 90, 97
 Samuel, 21, 62

INDEX

METCALF, John, 15, 19, 33, 34, 64
METCALFE, John, 35
MIDDLEMORE, Dr., 6, 11, 28, 34, 36
MIDER, George, 77, 81
MILES,
 Peter, 75, 82, 84, 101
 Thomas, 17, 20, 41, 47
MILLER,
 Joanna, 26
 Johannes, 76, 81, 90, 93, 103
 Thomas, 14, 18
MILLS,
 Robert, 43
 Thomas, 73
MITCHELL,
 Kent, 77
 Thomas, 43, 49
MOALE, John, 63, 67, 71, 76, 80, 85, 89, 101
MOLE, John, 12
MONK, Renaldo, 15, 19, 23
MONTGOMERY,
 Patrick, 39, 44, 49, 59
MOORE, John, 40, 46, 52
MORGAIN, Joseph, 41
MORGAN,
 David, 61, 66
 Joseph, 17, 21, 47, 53, 57, 61, 66, 69
MORTON, Frog, 98
MURPHEY, William, 18
MURPHY, William, 14
MURRAY,
 Josephus, 5, 9, 13, 17, 18, 36, 39, 42, 43, 48, 49, 53, 54, 58, 62, 63, 66, 70, 74, 75, 80, 86, 99, 100, 101

MURREY, Josephus, 85
MURRY, Joseph, 77, 81, 88
MYERS,
 George, 26, 75, 80, 85, 99, 100, 103
 Jacob, 75, 79, 82, 85, 87, 89, 92, 93

-N-
NAUGLE, Henry, 104
NEAVE, Timothy, 74
NELSON, Ambrose, 2, 3
NEWSOME, John, 4
NICHOLLS, Nathan, 75, 84, 85, 87, 94
NICHOLSON,
 Nathan, 87, 88, 92, 94, 98
 William, 84, 87
NICKOLS, Nathan, 20
NISBETT, Thomas, 21
NORMAN, George, 1
NORRIS,
 Benjamin, 15, 19, 23, 45, 51, 56, 60, 64, 72
 Edward, 27, 39, 78, 82
 James, 82
 John, 73
 Joseph, 16, 20, 24, 27, 40, 45, 51, 65, 69, 73, 75, 78, 80
NORTON, John, 5
NORWOOD, Samuel, 94, 95, 101
NULL, Anthony, 91, 97

-O-
OATES, Jacob, 22
OGDEN, Amos, 91, 92, 93
OGG, George, 10, 15, 19, 23, 26, 39, 44, 50, 55, 59, 63, 67, 71
ONION,
 Mr., 47
 Stephen, 33
 Zaccheus Barret, 13, 17, 69
ORGAN, Mathew, 1
ORRICH, Nicholas, 71
ORRICK,
 N., 51

Nicholas, 23, 38, 40, 45, 50, 56, 60, 64, 67, 76, 80, 85, 89
OSBORN, James, 24
OSBOURN, William, 4
OSBURN, Joseph, 92, 94
OWENS,
 Richard, 5
 Robert, 29
OWINGS,
 Bale, 80, 83
 Christopher, 76
 John Cockey, 80, 82, 85, 87, 89
 Joseph, 45
 Samuel, 10, 11, 15, 23, 26, 37, 39, 44, 50, 55, 76, 77, 80, 83, 85, 89, 90, 92, 93, 95, 100
 Widow, 14, 18, 19, 23, 43, 45, 49, 50, 54, 56, 67, 71, 81, 89, 93, 99

-P-
PACA,
 Aquila, 28
 Aquilla, 11
 Capt., 19, 45, 51, 56, 64
 John, 33, 34, 35, 37
 Mr., 6
 Mrs., 7
PAIN, Beaver, 45, 50, 51, 55, 56
PAINE,
 Beaver, 15, 19, 22, 23, 59, 60, 64, 71, 72
PAIRPOINT, Charles, 37
PARISH, William, 39, 55
PARKER, John, 16, 20, 22, 39, 41, 47, 61, 65, 69, 73, 80, 91, 99
PARRISH,
 Edward, 38
 John, 9
 William, 14, 18, 22, 35, 39, 42, 44, 48, 49, 54, 58, 59, 62, 63, 67, 71, 78

INDEX

PARTRIDGE, Dom:
  Bucklar, 34
PATTERSON,
  George, 77
  Robert, 43, 49, 54
PAUL, John, 104
PAYN, Beaver, 50, 55
PAYNE, Beaver, 63
PEARCE, William, 41, 47, 48, 52, 53, 57, 61, 66
PECKET, George, 3
PEDDICOAT, John, 34
PEERSON, Simon, 3
PENN, John, 23, 44, 50, 55
PERKIN, William, 41
PERKINS,
  Reuben, 25, 78
  Reubin, 15, 19, 72
  William, 9, 12
PERRIGOE,
  Joseph, 76, 80, 83
  William, 103, 104
PETICOAT,
  William, 11
PETTICOAT,
  Dorsey, 32
PETTICOATE,
  Dorsey, 30
PHELPS,
  James, 64
  Thomas, 9
PHILIPS,
  Francis, 26
  James, 45, 51, 76, 78
PHILLIPS,
  Francis, 17
  James, 28, 72
  Mr., 64
PHILPOT,
  Brian, 16
  Mrs., 77, 81, 83
PHILPOTT,
  Brian, 20, 24
  Mrs., 100
PICKET,
  Heathcoat, 53
  Heathcot, 69
  Heathcote, 17, 41, 42, 48, 57, 58, 61, 62, 66
PICKETT,
  Heathcoat, 35, 53
  Heathcot, 37
  William, 55
PIERCE, William, 21, 69
PIKE, William, 31
PILES, John, 39, 44
PITT, John, 26
PITTS,
  John, 77, 83, 86, 88, 92, 100
  Lewis, 100
PLOWAMN, Jonathan, 70
PLOWMAN,
  Jonathan, 58, 62, 66
  Mr., 26
POCOCK, Daniel, 61, 65
POE, David, 93, 94, 95
PONTANY, William, 49
PONTENY, William, 39, 43
PORTER,
  John Mercer, 94, 98
  Robert, 104
POWELL, Benjamin, 43, 49, 67, 70
PRESBURY,
  George, 37, 39, 43, 49, 54, 59, 63
  George C., 94
  George Gouldsmith, 98
  Joseph, 14, 18, 22
  William, 18
  William Robinson, 76
PRESTON,
  Daniel, 34, 36, 50, 55
  James, 2, 32, 36
PRICE,
  Aquila, 100
  Aquilla, 77, 81, 83
  Benjamin, 29
  John, 13, 39, 42, 48, 53, 58, 70, 77, 81, 83, 89, 98, 100, 104
  Mordecai, 17, 20, 25, 29, 42, 48, 53, 70, 74, 79, 82, 84, 92, 94, 97
  Stephen, 13, 17, 25, 39, 42, 43, 48, 49, 53, 54, 58, 59, 63, 67, 70, 75, 80, 89, 91, 98
  Steven, 54
  William, 98
PRITCHARD,
  James, 20, 24, 47, 52, 57, 60, 65, 68, 72
  Obediah, 14, 31, 54, 58, 70
  William, 2

-Q-

QUINE, William, 21, 61, 66

-R-

RANDALL,
  Christopher, 7, 12, 34
  William, 83
RANDELL,
  John, 37
  William, 86
RATTENBURY, John, 31
RAVEN, Luke, 7
RAWLINGS, Daniel, 8
RAY, Hugh, 13, 17, 61, 66, 69
READ, John, 81, 89, 93, 99
REESTON, Edward, 10
REISTER, John, 13, 70, 74, 82, 84
RENSHAW,
  John, 32
  Thomas, 20, 25, 33
RICE, James, 96, 99
RICHARDS,
  Nicholas, 80, 82
  Richard, 14, 18, 63, 67, 70
RICHARDSON,
  Lawrence, 1
  Nath., 33
  Nathaniel, 32
  Richard, 29
  Thomas, 31, 33, 47, 52, 57, 60, 65, 69, 73
RIDGELEY,
  Charles, 30
  John, 58
RIDGELY,
  Charles, 10, 39, 82, 84, 101
  John, 35, 38

INDEX

RIGBIE,
  James, 57
  Nathan, 24, 30
RIGDON,
  George, 22, 32, 44, 50, 55, 59, 63, 71
  Stephen, 21
  Thomas Baker, 25
  William, 38
RISER, John, 84
RISTEAU,
  George, 15, 44, 50, 55, 59, 64, 67, 71, 76, 77, 80, 81, 83, 85, 89, 100
  Isaac, 13, 17, 43, 45, 48, 49, 53, 54, 57, 59, 62, 66, 69
  Issac, 42
  John, 76, 80, 85, 89, 98
  Thomas, 100
  Widow, 25
RISTER, John, 79, 87
RISTON,
  Edward, 7
  John, 26
ROBERT, John, 4
ROBERTS,
  John, 4, 10
  Levin, 21
ROBERTSON,
  Jonas, 10
  Richard, 34
  Robert, 9
ROBINSON,
  Charles, 17, 25, 98, 103
  Daniel, 77
  Francis, 1
  Jonas, 9
  William, 3, 26
ROCKHOLD,
  Charles, 4
ROCKWELL,
  Charles, 11
ROGER, Benjamin, 86
ROGERS,
  B., 26
  Benjamin, 22, 25, 27, 74, 75, 76, 79, 80, 81, 82, 85, 89, 90, 91, 95, 97, 98, 99, 100, 101
  Charles, 79, 84, 86, 90, 97
  John, 10, 12, 77
  Mr., 78
  William, 44, 49, 55, 58
RUFF, Richard, 33
RUMSEY, Benjamin, 73
RUTE, Daniel, 43
RUTH, Moses, 38, 40, 45, 51
RUTLAGE, Abraham, 16, 73
RUTTER, Thomas, 96

-S-

SAMPSON, Richard, 101, 103
SAMSON, Richard, 2, 3
SANDERS, Thomas, 43
SATER, Henry, 86, 88
SATYR, Henry, 10
SAVORY, William, 11, 38
SCHOLFIELD, John, 18, 22
SCHOOLFIELD, John, 13
SCOTT,
  Abraham, 80, 82, 85
  Aquila, 36
  Daniel, 6, 16, 46, 52
  James, 36
  Widow, 22, 36, 44, 50, 55, 59, 63, 71
SEAL, James, 43
SEWELL,
  Christopher, 26, 27, 74, 79, 84, 91, 97
  Joshua, 45, 50, 56
SHAMMEDINE, John, 19
SHARPE, Thomas, 24
SHAUL, Joseph, 101
SHAW,
  Daniel, 81, 93, 95, 96, 101
  Thomas Knight, 95
  Thomas Knight Smith, 92
SHEA, Thomas, 29
SHEAPARD, Nath., 30
SHEPHARD, Nathaniel, 29
SHEPHERD,
  John, 75, 96, 101
  Widow, 20, 25, 39
SHEPPARD, Widow, 41, 47, 61, 66
SHEPPERD, Widow, 16, 65, 69, 73
SHEREDINE, Thomas, 12, 17, 29, 30, 34, 65, 69, 73
SHERMANDINE, John, 15
SHIELDS, David, 92
SHOWERS, John, 95
SHY, Thomas, 28
SILVER, James, 59, 63
SIMKIN, John, 55
SIMKINS, John, 39, 45, 50, 56, 59, 63
SIMMONS,
  Charles, 6
  George, 22
SIMPKINS, John, 44, 50, 55
SKINNER, John, 40, 46, 52, 56, 60, 64, 68, 72, 87, 89, 91
SLADE,
  Ezekiel, 41, 47
  Josiah, 39
  Josias, 16, 20, 27, 35, 41, 47, 61, 65, 69, 73, 75, 93, 95
  Mr., 96
  William, 16, 20, 93, 95, 96, 101
SLAID,
  Josias, 80, 91, 98, 99
  Mr., 101
SLIGH, Thomas, 12
SMITH,
  Bacon, 75, 81
  George, 1
  Isgrig, 77, 83, 90, 93
  Isgrigs, 100
  John Addison, 13, 69
  Joseph, 43, 45, 47, 52
  Ralph, 19
  Walter, 26, 77, 83, 88, 90, 93, 100
  William, 6, 9, 16, 20, 28, 30, 34, 35, 37, 38, 39, 46, 51, 56, 68, 73
SMITHSON, David, 103
SNIDER, Michael, 96, 101, 104

INDEX

SNOWDEN, Francis, 94, 96
SOLLARS, High, 20
SOLLERS,
  Elisha, 104
  Francis, 23
  High, 16, 24, 68
  Hugh, 60, 65
  Thomas, 27
SPEIER, Thomas, 33
SPENCER,
  Zachariah, 12, 32, 33
SPENSER,
  Zachariah, 9
STANBURY, Daniel, 30
STANDEFORD,
  William, 99
STANDIFORD,
  John, 81, 83, 86, 88, 90, 93, 95, 96
  Skelton, 32, 81, 83, 100
  William, 31, 32, 80
STANSBURY,
  Daniel, 33
  Dixon, 80, 82, 85, 87, 89, 92, 95, 98
  Edmund, 86, 88, 90, 93
  Joseph, 94, 96, 97
  Luke, 7, 8, 11, 12, 17, 32, 41, 47, 53, 57, 69
  Mr., 35
  Samuel, 12, 41, 48, 53, 57
  Thomas, 6, 16, 20, 24, 40, 46, 52, 56, 60, 65, 68, 72
STARKEY,
  James, 10
  Jonathan, 18, 40, 42, 48, 53, 58
  Joseph, 10
STARNSBORO,
  Tobias, 2
STARNSBURY, Luke, 5
STENSON, William, 94, 96

STEPHENSON, Widow, 3
STERETT, James, 84
STERRETT, James, 87
STEVENSON,
  Dr., 76, 80, 85, 89
  John, 79, 84, 86, 90, 97
  Joshua, 84, 86, 90, 91
  Richard, 36
  William, 78
STEWART, George, 73, 74, 77, 78
STINCECOMB,
  Nathaniel, 18, 22
STINCHCOMB,
  Nathaniel, 36, 103
STINCHICOMB, John, 37
STOCDALL, Edward, 31
STOCKSDALE, Edward, 36, 38
STODDARD, David, 101
STOKES,
  George, 30
  John, 2
  Wells, 10
STOKSDALL, Edward, 36
STORM, George, 101, 103
STOUFFER, Henry, 101, 104
STOXDILL, Edward, 38
STRAWBELL,
  Zachariah, 80, 91
STRAWBILL,
  Zachariah, 75
STRAWBLE, Zachariah, 98
STUMP, Henry, 22, 43, 52, 57, 60, 65
SUTTON,
  Christopher, 66, 69
  Joseph, 21, 42, 48, 53, 69, 80, 82, 85, 87, 89, 92, 95, 99
SWINGLE, John, 93, 95

-T-

TALBOT,
  Edward, 38
  James, 41, 47
  Widow, 15, 19, 41,

45, 47, 51, 64
TALBOTT,
  Benjamin, 89, 91
  Edmond, 5
  Edmund, 19
  Edward, 85, 87, 89
  John, 24, 97, 101
  Thomas, 20, 24, 75, 80, 91, 98
  Widow, 20, 22, 23, 65, 73
TANNER, George, 104
TAYLER, John, 34
TAYLOR,
  James, 15, 19, 24, 40, 46, 51, 56, 60, 64, 68, 72
  John, 24, 57, 61, 65
  Joseph, 13, 18, 22, 36, 39, 42, 48, 54, 58, 62
  Lawrence, 4
TEAL,
  Edward, 89, 92, 93
  Emanuel, 14, 18, 31
  Emmanuel, 44, 49, 50, 54, 55
  Emmel, 43
TEALE, Widow, 12
TEALL, Emanuel, 23
TEVIS,
  Peter, 91, 92, 94
  Robert, 13, 42
THARP, Edward, 15, 19, 45, 51
THOMAS, David, 23, 31, 34
THOMPSON,
  Andrew, 38
  Robert, 43
  Thomas, 40, 43, 49, 54
THORNBOROUGH,
  Rowland, 1
THORNTON, George, 81, 84, 101
THORP, Edward, 15, 19, 20, 23, 45, 51, 64
THORPE, Edward, 12, 24
TIERS, Robert, 41
TIMMONDS, John, 22
TIPTON,
  Bryan, 103
  Jonathan, 3, 91, 96, 97
  Joshua, 104
  Thomas, 17, 25, 29, 30
TIVIS, Robert, 41,

115

INDEX

42, 62, 66, 70
TOD, Lancelot, 3
TODD, Thomas, 12, 16, 20, 24, 60, 65, 68, 72, 104
TOLLEY,
  James, 31
  Mr., 17, 41, 47, 53, 57, 69
  Thomas, 4, 10
  Walter, 13, 17, 31, 38, 39, 43, 47, 49, 54, 59, 62, 63, 66, 70
TOULSON,
  Zachariah, 26
TOWSON,
  Ezekiel, 27, 83, 100
  William, 40
  Zekiel, 77, 88
TRACEY,
  Tague, 38
  Teague, 29
TRACY, Teagoe, 2
TRAPNELL,
  William, 43, 49, 54
TREADWAY,
  Mr., 84
  Thomas, 33, 37
TREDAWAY,
  Daniel, 56, 60, 64
  Thomas, 56, 60
TREDWAY,
  Daniel, 45, 51, 56
  Mr., 81, 101
  Thomas, 51
TREMBLE, William, 97, 103
TROTTEN, Luke, 5, 10, 36

-V-

VANHORN, Gabriel P., 95, 96
VANSICKLE, Henry, 76
VAUGHAN,
  Christopher, 39, 42, 75
  Richard, 42, 48, 53, 58, 62, 66, 70

-W-

WAGERS, Benjamin, 13, 18
WAKEMAN,
  Dr., 11, 12, 14, 28, 42, 48, 54, 62, 67, 70
  Edward, 31
WAKERMAN, Dr., 58
WALKER, Charles, 96, 101
WALLACE, Samuel, 16, 24, 44, 46, 49, 51, 56, 60, 64
WALTHAM, Thomas, 67
WALTHOM, Thomas, 70
WARD, Edward, 40, 46, 51, 56, 60
WASHINGTON, Phillip, 4
WATKINS, Joseph, 40, 41
WEBB, Samuel, 24, 46, 51, 68
WEBSTER,
  Isaac, 35, 40, 46, 51, 60, 64, 68
  James, 15, 68, 72, 98
  John, 6, 8, 15, 19, 24, 28, 37, 43, 45, 46, 49, 51, 54, 56, 60, 64, 68
  John Lee, 74
  Michael, 28, 37
  Samuel, 28, 35
WEEKS, Thomas, 5
WELLS,
  Alexander, 19, 23, 76
  Charles, 8, 10, 12, 81, 84, 101
  Francis, 26, 62, 66, 74, 87, 101
  George, 1, 2
  James, 10, 11, 38
  John, 57
  Richard, 9, 12, 13, 17, 66, 69
WELSH, James, 35
WEST,
  John, 41, 47, 57, 61
  Robert, 12, 29, 43
WETHERAL, Henry, 63, 67
WETHERALL, Henry, 10
WHEELER,
  Benjamin, 8, 75, 80, 86, 89, 91, 97, 98

Greenberry, 97, 103
Ignatius, 22, 34, 59, 63, 67, 71, 77
Mordecai, 103
Nathan, 99, 103
Samuel, 22
Thomas, 14, 18, 44, 50, 71
WHIPS, Benjamin, 42, 48, 53, 58, 62
WHITEACRE, John, 31
WHITEHEAD,
  Francis, 3
  Widow, 12
WHITTACRE, Peter, 20, 24
WHITTAKER, Mark, 4
WIESNER, Matthias, 101
WILEY, Luke, 32
WILKINSON,
  Stephen, 6
  William, 2
WILLING, John, 4
WILLMOTT, John, 33, 36
WILLSON, Benkid, 43
WILMOT,
  John, 3, 17
  Richard, 43, 49, 51, 54, 56, 59, 60, 63, 64
WILMOTT,
  John, 31, 99
  Richard, 38
  Robert, 95
WILSON,
  Benjamin Kidd, 39, 41, 59, 62
  Henry, 60, 65
  John, 25, 81
  William, 14, 16, 20, 24, 70
WISELY, John, 6
WOOD,
  Isaac, 33, 37, 40, 41, 43, 45, 49, 78
  William, 11
WOODEN,
  John, 39, 42
  Solomon, 10, 104
  Stephen, 75, 89, 98
WOODLAND, Jonathan, 76
WOODWAD, John, 52
WOODWARD, John, 46, 56
WORTHINGTON,
  Charles, 34, 36
  Samuel, 26, 58, 96,

INDEX

101
  William, 37
WRIGHT,
  John, 29
  Thomas, 6
  William, 3
WYDLEY,
    Greenberry,
    101
WYLEY,
  Greenberry, 96
  John, 34
  William, 96

-Y-
YOE, James, 25
YOUNG,
  Benjamin, 15,
    19, 23, 71
  Col., 14, 18,
    22, 44, 50,
    55, 57, 59,
    71
  Henry, 14, 18,
    22, 43, 49,
    54, 58, 62,
    67, 70
  John, 47, 53
  John Tully, 104
  Samuel, 81, 84,
    101
  William, 14,
    31, 33, 34,
    63, 67, 71

Other books by the author:

A Closer Look at St. John's Parish Registers [Baltimore County, Maryland], 1701-1801
A Collection of Maryland Church Records
A Guide to Genealogical Research in Maryland: 5th Edition, Revised and Enlarged
Abstracts of the Ledgers and Accounts of the Bush Store and Rock Run Store, 1759-1771
Abstracts of the Orphans Court Proceedings of Harford County, 1778-1800
Abstracts of Wills, Harford County, Maryland, 1800-1805
Baltimore City [Maryland] Deaths and Burials, 1834-1840
Baltimore County, Maryland, Overseers of Roads, 1693-1793
Bastardy Cases in Baltimore County, Maryland, 1673-1783
Bastardy Cases in Harford County, Maryland, 1774-1844
Bible and Family Records of Harford County, Maryland Families: Volume V
Children of Harford County: Indentures and Guardianships, 1801-1830
Colonial Delaware Soldiers and Sailors, 1638-1776
*Colonial Families of the Eastern Shore of Maryland
Volumes 5, 6, 7, 8, 9, 11, 12, 13, 14, and 16*
Colonial Maryland Soldiers and Sailors, 1634-1734
Dr. John Archer's First Medical Ledger, 1767-1769, Annotated Abstracts
Early Anglican Records of Cecil County
*Early Harford Countians, Individuals Living in Harford County, Maryland in Its Formative Years
Volume 1: A to K, Volume 2: L to Z, and Volume 3: Supplement*
Harford County Taxpayers in 1870, 1872 and 1883
Harford County, Maryland Divorce Cases, 1827-1912: An Annotated Index
Heirs and Legatees of Harford County, Maryland, 1774-1802
Heirs and Legatees of Harford County, Maryland, 1802-1846
Inhabitants of Baltimore County, Maryland, 1763-1774
Inhabitants of Cecil County, Maryland, 1649-1774
Inhabitants of Harford County, Maryland, 1791-1800
Inhabitants of Kent County, Maryland, 1637-1787
*Joseph A. Pennington & Co., Havre De Grace, Maryland Funeral Home Records:
Volume II, 1877-1882, 1893-1900*
Maryland Bible Records, Volume 1: Baltimore and Harford Counties
Maryland Bible Records, Volume 2: Baltimore and Harford Counties
Maryland Bible Records, Volume 3: Carroll County
Maryland Bible Records, Volume 4: Eastern Shore
Maryland Deponents, 1634-1799
Maryland Deponents: Volume 3, 1634-1776
*Maryland Public Service Records, 1775-1783: A Compendium of Men and Women of
Maryland Who Rendered Aid in Support of the American Cause against
Great Britain during the Revolutionary War*
*Marylanders to Carolina: Migration of Marylanders to
North Carolina and South Carolina prior to 1800*

Marylanders to Kentucky, 1775-1825
Methodist Records of Baltimore City, Maryland: Volume 1, 1799-1829
Methodist Records of Baltimore City, Maryland: Volume 2, 1830-1839
Methodist Records of Baltimore City, Maryland: Volume 3, 1840-1850 (East City Station)
More Maryland Deponents, 1716-1799
More Marylanders to Carolina: Migration of Marylanders to North Carolina and South Carolina prior to 1800
More Marylanders to Kentucky, 1778-1828
Outpensioners of Harford County, Maryland, 1856-1896
Presbyterian Records of Baltimore City, Maryland, 1765-1840
Quaker Records of Baltimore and Harford Counties, Maryland, 1801-1825
Quaker Records of Northern Maryland, 1716-1800
Quaker Records of Southern Maryland, 1658-1800
Revolutionary Patriots of Anne Arundel County, Maryland
Revolutionary Patriots of Baltimore Town and Baltimore County, 1775-1783
Revolutionary Patriots of Calvert and St. Mary's Counties, Maryland, 1775-1783
Revolutionary Patriots of Caroline County, Maryland, 1775-1783
Revolutionary Patriots of Cecil County, Maryland
Revolutionary Patriots of Charles County, Maryland, 1775-1783
Revolutionary Patriots of Delaware, 1775-1783
Revolutionary Patriots of Dorchester County, Maryland, 1775-1783
Revolutionary Patriots of Frederick County, Maryland, 1775-1783
Revolutionary Patriots of Harford County, Maryland, 1775-1783
Revolutionary Patriots of Kent and Queen Anne's Counties
Revolutionary Patriots of Lancaster County, Pennsylvania
Revolutionary Patriots of Maryland, 1775-1783: A Supplement
Revolutionary Patriots of Maryland, 1775-1783: Second Supplement
Revolutionary Patriots of Montgomery County, Maryland, 1776-1783
Revolutionary Patriots of Prince George's County, Maryland, 1775-1783
Revolutionary Patriots of Talbot County, Maryland, 1775-1783
Revolutionary Patriots of Worcester and Somerset Counties, Maryland, 1775-1783
Revolutionary Patriots of Washington County, Maryland, 1776-1783
St. George's (Old Spesutia) Parish, Harford County, Maryland: Church and Cemetery Records, 1820-1920
St. John's and St. George's Parish Registers, 1696-1851
Survey Field Book of David and William Clark in Harford County, Maryland, 1770-1812
The Crenshaws of Kentucky, 1800-1995
The Delaware Militia in the War of 1812
Union Chapel United Methodist Church Cemetery Tombstone Inscriptions, Wilna, Harford County, Maryland

www.ingramcontent.com/pod-product-compliance
Lightning Source LLC
Chambersburg PA
CBHW070507100426
42743CB00010B/1784